Palgrave Studies on Chinese Education in a Global Perspective

Series Editors
Fred Dervin
Department of Education
University of Helsinki
Helsinki, Finland

Xiangyun Du
College of Education
Qatar University
Doha, Qatar

The transformation of China into a global super-power is often attributed to the country's robust education system and this series seeks to provide a comprehensive, in-depth understanding of the development of Chinese education on a global scale. The books in this series will analyze and problematize the revolutions, reforms, innovations and transformations of Chinese education that are often misunderstood or misrepresented beyond its own borders and will examine the changes in Chinese education over the past 30 years and the issues as well as challenges that the future of Chinese education faces. For more information or to submit a proposal please contact Rebecca Wyde (rebecca.wyde@palgrave.com).

Mei Yuan • Fred Dervin
Sude • Ning Chen

Change and Exchange in Global Education

Learning with Chinese Stories of Interculturality

Mei Yuan
Minzu University of China
Beijing, China

Sude
School of Education
Minzu University of China
Beijing, China

Fred Dervin
Department of Education
University of Helsinki
Helsinki, Finland

Ning Chen
School of Experimental Arts
Tianjin Academy of Fine Arts
Tianjin, China

ISSN 2945-6576 ISSN 2945-6584 (electronic)
Palgrave Studies on Chinese Education in a Global Perspective
ISBN 978-3-031-12769-4 ISBN 978-3-031-12770-0 (eBook)
https://doi.org/10.1007/978-3-031-12770-0

© The Editor(s) (if applicable) and The Author(s), under exclusive licence to Springer Nature Switzerland AG, part of Springer Nature 2022

This work is subject to copyright. All rights are solely and exclusively licensed by the Publisher, whether the whole or part of the material is concerned, specifically the rights of translation, reprinting, reuse of illustrations, recitation, broadcasting, reproduction on microfilms or in any other physical way, and transmission or information storage and retrieval, electronic adaptation, computer software, or by similar or dissimilar methodology now known or hereafter developed.

The use of general descriptive names, registered names, trademarks, service marks, etc. in this publication does not imply, even in the absence of a specific statement, that such names are exempt from the relevant protective laws and regulations and therefore free for general use.

The publisher, the authors, and the editors are safe to assume that the advice and information in this book are believed to be true and accurate at the date of publication. Neither the publisher nor the authors or the editors give a warranty, expressed or implied, with respect to the material contained herein or for any errors or omissions that may have been made. The publisher remains neutral with regard to jurisdictional claims in published maps and institutional affiliations.

This Palgrave Macmillan imprint is published by the registered company Springer Nature Switzerland AG.

The registered company address is: Gewerbestrasse 11, 6330 Cham, Switzerland

This book is dedicated to J.P.D. and Eddy.

ACKNOWLEDGEMENTS

Change and Exchange in Intercultural Communication Education— Learning from Chinese Stories of Interculturality benefitted from the precious help of Yuyin Liang from Minzu University of China. Her support is greatly appreciated. The authors remain solely responsible for any remaining errors or omissions.

We also thank our students in China and Finland for their very valuable contribution.

Contents

1 Introduction: Why *'Chinese'* Stories of Interculturality?   1
   Fred Dervin

2 Approaching Interculturality: Culture and Civilization as Discursive and Reflexive Tools   25

3 Exploring and Explaining Experiences of Interculturality   55

4 'Doing' Interculturality Together   77

5 Making Interculturality Work Together, as Group/Community Members   101

6 Learning to 'Do' Interculturality: *Setting Objectives for Oneself*   125

7 Pondering over Language and Interculturality   153

| 8 | Interim Conclusions
Fred Dervin | 179 |

Full List of Discourse Instruments 187

Index 197

List of Figures

Fig. 1.1	Interculturality as an octopus	5
Fig. 1.2	'Ethnic culture' in a Chinese bookstore	6
Fig. 2.1	A banner with the word civilization in Chinese being displayed on the streets of Beijing	26
Fig. 2.2	The word *culture* in Chinese and English used on a banner to promote sports at Minzu University of China	27
Fig. 2.3	The word *culture* in Chinese in a bookstore	28
Fig. 2.4	Book entitled 中国历史常识 ('general knowledge of Chinese literature') by Zheng Zhenduo (2019), published by Tiandi Press	33
Fig. 2.5	An example of 文化词汇: *YYDS* in Chinese stands for 永远的神 (Yǒngyuǎn de shén), an expression used to show great admiration for someone and translates as *eternal/forever God*. YYDS are the first letters of each word from the Pinyin of 永远的神	38
Fig. 2.6	Civilization is the most beautiful scenery	44
Fig. 2.7	A person wearing a coat that reads OTHERS—Happiness to make you sweet enough trials make	45
Fig. 2.8	An example of exhibits of 文化创意产业, with a focus on Chinese Minzu elements	47
Fig. 2.9	Lady wearing a Hanfu dress	48
Fig. 2.10	Chapter summary (culture and civilization)	50
Fig. 3.1	Chapter summary (free your mind, empathy and meeting the other)	72
Fig. 4.1	The words 自由平等 (freedom and equality), 爱国 (patriotism), 富强 (prosperity), 和谐 (harmony), 文明和谐 (civilization and harmony) on a street panel in Chaoyang district (Beijing)	79

xii   LIST OF FIGURES

Fig. 4.2	A street sign containing the word 和 (harmony). Erdos, Inner Mongolia	80
Fig. 4.3	*A diversified and harmonious world.* Banner at the campus of Minzu University of China	82
Fig. 4.4	A biographical notice about Fei Xiaotong (费孝通) at Minzu University Museum	85
Fig. 4.5	The discourse instrument of 知行合一 on a Chinese campus	93
Fig. 4.6	Chapter summary	97
Fig. 5.1	The innovation and entrepreneurship centre of Minzu University of China, with the logo 56 创 (to create/entrepreneurship) in reference to the 56 Minzu groups of China	103
Fig. 5.2	Commemorative stamps for Minzu University of China, celebrating the 'Great Unity of the Chinese Nation'	104
Fig. 5.3	The words *Happy* and *Happiness* are often seen or heard in Chinese and/or English in China, as is the case here on a street vendor car	111
Fig. 5.4	Chinese initiatives for (glocal) interculturality	120
Fig. 5.5	Interculturality and togetherness	121
Fig. 5.6	Learning togetherness in the Chinese context	121
Fig. 6.1	References to Mencius, Xunzi and the Analects by Confucius on a street panel. The big characters on both sides of the panel are 礼 (Li, i.e. ritual) and 智 (Zhi, wisdom, knowledge)	126
Fig. 6.2	The character for 仁 (*rén*, benevolence) on a rock	129
Fig. 6.3	Chapter summary (looking at oneself)	144
Fig. 6.4	Group 1: Try to put yourself in their shoes	146
Fig. 6.5	Group 2: Perfect	146
Fig. 6.6	Group 3: Think cautiously	147
Fig. 6.7	Group 4: The octopus	148
Fig. 7.1	An example of written Uyghur (From Minzu University of China Museum)	156
Fig. 7.2	Northern Yi Dialect (From Minzu University of China Museum)	157
Fig. 7.3	Chapter summary (language and interculturality)	173

CHAPTER 1

Introduction: Why *'Chinese'* Stories of Interculturality?

Fred Dervin

This book is the result of three years of intense cooperation between the authors in China and Finland. Several articles, chapters and books have preceded the publication of this book, on which it is built (e.g. Yuan et al., 2020; Dervin & Yuan, 2021; Dervin et al., 2022). What we tried to achieve together was to open up global discussions around the 'right to speak' about interculturality, to offer new opportunities to listen to other voices and 'revitalize' interculturality in global education. Up to a point, we have been successful at doing so. However, we always felt that there is more to do to enrich our own ways of unthinking and rethinking interculturality and to share them with our readers. This book represents another stepping stone, digging deeper into what will be referred to as 'Chinese stories of interculturality'. After having identified problems and short-term solutions to interculturality in communication and education, we now offer to explore real complements to what has already been proposed in the field worldwide.

As the principal initiator and 'engineer' of this important project, and as a scholar from the 'West'[1] working with colleagues and friends from Mainland China, in what follows, I reflect on why this book was needed and what it aims for. In my engagement with Chinese colleagues and students, I have often noted specific ways of talking about interculturality in English as a global language. While comparing words, phrases and utterances not only in Chinese, English but also Finnish, French, German and Swedish, I realized that there were many more layers of connotations and meanings than I expected. *My interculturality is not always your interculturality...* How could we thus communicate around interculturality without looking into this important aspect of interculturality? This book is provided as one answer to this question.

Interculturality 'Octopusied'

A few days ago, a friend sent me beautiful images of bright star clusters and distant galaxies that her partner, an amateur 'astrophographer', had taken. Although, like everyone else, I am aware that there is a world 'out there'—composed of stars, constellations, milky ways, and so on, in all my naivety, I was speechless (and jealous!): my friend's partner had access to such beautiful and complex-looking elements that my untrained eyes never even paid attention to when I have stared at the sky at night. All these deep-space objects on the pictures that she shared made me think of the topic of this book that we have put together with my teams at the University of Helsinki and Minzu University of China. If I could summarize what this book is about in a few words, I would say that it deals with having access to knowledge about interculturality that is invisible to our eyes but that is out there. Our book is like *a telescope*, forming magnified images of far-off objects, and as we shall see, objects that have been brushed aside, ignored and disregarded, while privileging forms of common sense about the notion, imposed on the world by powerful voices.

In order to explain the importance of using investigative tools like a telescope for interculturality, I will start by using another metaphor to reflect on the complexity of interculturality as an object of scholarship and education—that of an octopus. Let us start with a quote from the French writer Victor Hugo (1866: 213) about the octopus:

---

[1] The word *the 'West'* will be systematically surrounded by inverted commas in the book to indicate that this notion represents a complex representation of powerful voices and ideologies in today's world. The 'West' is not located in specific parts of the world. It symbolizes omnipresent and dominant forces in most economic-political-academic-discursive spheres globally.

1 INTRODUCTION: WHY '*CHINESE*' STORIES OF INTERCULTURALITY?

> If terror were the object of... creation, nothing could be imagined more perfect than the devil-fish... This irregular mass advances slowly towards you. Suddenly it opens, and eight radii issue abruptly from around a face with two eyes. These radii are alive: their undulation is like lambent flames... A terrible expansion!... Its folds strangle, its contact paralyses. It has an aspect like gangrened or scabrous flesh. It is a monstrous embodiment of disease... Underneath each of [its] feelers range two rows of pustules, decreasing in size... They are cartilaginous substances, cylindrical, horny and livid... A glutinous mass, endowed with a malignant will, what can be more horrible?

This terrifying quote gives us a sense of how this creature has been (mis-)perceived in certain parts of the world: "like gangrened or scabrous flesh. It is a monstrous embodiment of disease"; "[it is] endowed with a malignant will, what can be more horrible?". In my comparison to interculturality, I am interested in two elements—leaving aside these subjective and sensationalist observations. The octopus is described as 'irregular mass', 'glutinous' (sticky, glue-like), with 'radii' (plural form of *radius*, a line extending from a circle) that are alive and rising and falling. I argue that the octopus metaphor can help us problematize how to deal with interculturality in a more global way, enabling us to look at it in its complexity and diversity. I have proposed elsewhere to *interculturalise interculturality* (e.g. Dervin & Jacobsson, 2021; see also Ferri, 2018) and I believe that the octopus metaphor can explain how we could (re)consider the position of interculturality and (maybe) how to deal with it in many and varied ways. This is the main objective of this book, taking into account Chinese perspectives.

Some words about the octopus, based on a summary of Mather (2019) and Smith (2021). The octopus is identified as a cephalopod and has been referred to as *singulare monstrum* (a unique monster) by Swedish naturalist and explorer Linnaeus who framed principles for defining species of organisms back in the eighteenth century. Most readers will have seen (pictures of) octopuses, however, as a reminder: an octopus is an eight-armed, soft-bodied mollusk. Octopuses can range in size from several metres arm span (e.g. the *Giant Pacific*) to the 2.5-centimetre long *octopus wolfi*. The arms of octopuses are covered in suckers, each with ten thousand neurons, which means that they can taste and smell, as well as demonstrate short-term memory. Their lifespan is short, from 1 to 4 years.

What are the specificities of the octopus? This will help us start reflect on interculturality. First and foremost, the octopus has 'intelligence' dispersed throughout its body, going beyond the 'human' body/brain division. As such an octopus brain contains around 500 million neurons—similar to a three-year old child; its eight arms have almost twice as many nerve cells as in its brain; its arms are partly self-directed, each representing somehow a 'thinking thing', different arms can thus execute different actions harmoniously—not as fixed movement; finally, its arms are partly *self*, partly *other*. Second, the octopus is an inquisitive, observant and friendly creature. As a sophisticated problem solver, it can learn and use tools and is able to, for example, negotiate mazes and unscrew jars containing food, manipulate half-coconut shells in ways that imply they are probing their shapes as much as using them, learn to turn off lights by squirting water at the bulbs. The octopus is also cunning and has a capacity for imitation but also deception. As a protean sea creature, it has the ability to colour-camouflage to match their surroundings by means of its layered screen of pixel-like skin cells. In other words, the octopus can 'see' with its skin. Norman et al. (2001) show for example that its biological plasticity can allow the 'mimic octopus' to imitate more than 15 animals by changing its colour and shape. Finally, since its boneless mass of soft tissue has no fixed shape, an octopus can for example, escape through small holes.

Back to interculturality now, another 'unique monster'. *Monster* here is not meant to be a derogatory word. The label is used ironically, bearing in mind that the word in English is from the Latin derivative *monere* which means *to remind, to admonish*, but also *to advise, to instruct* and *to teach*. Like the octopus, one could say that interculturality has involved sophisticated problem-solving over the decades that it has been researched and used in global education (amongst others). At first sight, the notion appears 'diverse' in the way it is constructed, discussed and expressed. Multiple solutions/strategies have been developed around it, in many and varied economic-political contexts. Often influenced by different, similar and overlapping ideologies (e.g. through supranational institutions like the UNESCO, OECD, see e.g. Ingoglia et al., 2021), solutions/strategies can be borrowed and/or mixed from/with other contexts. Figure 1.1 is a projection of interculturality as an octopus.

Globally, interculturality has different arms, different 'thinking things'. One notices similar shared goals (symbolized by the head of the octopus) with for example, *diversity, inclusion, tolerance, unity, social justice* and *human rights* at its core. However, the way these are conceptualized, defined and understood glocally, as well as the different beliefs and actions that go with them, will differ politically, economically and ideologically (see *partly self, partly other* for the octopus radii). I have included seven different perspectives in the figure (see Dervin & Jacobsson, 2021; Ibelema, 2021; Kulich et al., 2020; Dervin & Yuan, 2021; Aman, 2017;

1 INTRODUCTION: WHY 'CHINESE' STORIES OF INTERCULTURALITY?

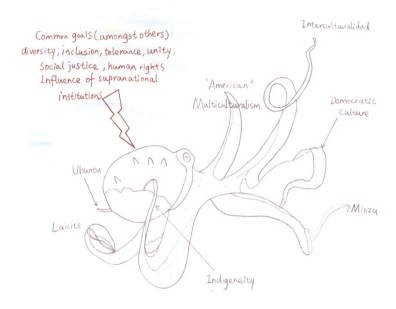

Fig. 1.1 Interculturality as an octopus

Ferri, 2018): (in alphabetical order) 'American' multiculturalism, democratic culture, indigineity, interculturalidad, laïcité, Minzu, Ubuntu.[2] We must bear in mind that many more such perspectives on interculturality are available.

---

[2] In an article published just as we were putting the last touch to this book, Baker (2021) 'introduced' the notion of *the transcultural* as an 'alternative' for *the intercultural* in research. The author (2021) claims that "the traditional metaphor of 'inter' for intercultural communication is no longer adequate and such communication is better approached as transcultural communication where borders are transcended, transgressed and in the process transformed". In a typical 'Western-centric' fashion (i.e. a 'Western' critique of 'Western' ideologies), with references only in English, the article represents a good example of 'epistemocentric myopa'. Replacing a word (*intercultural*) with another (*transcultural*) does not make a difference if the ideological foundations (and the critiques that go with them) remain the same. As much as the intercultural is not a single entity worldwide, the transcultural, in all its multilingual, geo-economic-political complexities, cannot be 'kidnapped' and turned into a doxic, simplified notion. Instead of rushing to dictate that *the intercultural* is this or that (as I did in the past) and *the transcultural* this or that, it is important to listen to how multiple voices from around the world (from students to people on the streets) problematize them. This applies to all the different 'arms' of the proposed octopus.

It is important to note that the use of different languages within and between these radii contributes to the complexity of interculturality. As such, language-thought might differ when one uses such concepts as ethnicity, exotic or tolerance in English and other languages—and this applies to the so-called West and to other parts of the world. Figure 1.2 shows an example for Chinese, where the idea of 民族 (Minzu) is translated as 'ethnic' in English. Although most dictionaries will indicate this word as a synonym (or 'nation', marginally 'race'), 民族 (Minzu) is much more than these 'equivalents', actually it refers to something else in the Chinese context: 56 groups of people, united and diverse in (at times) languages, cultures, and worldviews, with a common history—that of the Chinese nation. One's Minzu is often asked for when filling in a form in China. It is also indicated in one's identity papers.

As aforementioned, in the West, many and varied ideologies are attached to interculturality, which are not necessarily understood and used the same way—or even not used at all in some parts of the 'West':

Fig. 1.2 'Ethnic culture' in a Chinese bookstore

- Canada: for example, *indigeneity*
- Finland: for example, *linguistic diversity (it is illegal to ask for people's ethnicity/race officially)*
- France: for example, *secularism (no 'difference')*
- Sweden: for example, *ethnic and linguistic diversity*
- UK: for example, *ethnic group*
- US: for example, *race.*

On a US form one might find the following categories (concerning race): *White; Black, African Am.; American Indian or Alaska Native; Asian Indian; Chinese; Filipino; Japanese; Korean; Vietnamese; Other Asian; Native Hawaiian; Guamanian or Chamorro; Samoart; Other Pacific Islander; Some other race.* In Britain, one might see the following categories being included when asking about someone's ethnic group: *White; English/Welsh/Scottish/Northern Irish/British; Irish; Gypsy or Irish Traveller; Any other White background; Mixed/multiple ethnic groups; White and Black Caribbean; White and Black African; White and Asian; Any other Mixed/multiple ethnic background.*

So, interculturality, like the octopus, represents, at first sight, paradigmatic, political, ideological, linguistic and conceptual plasticity. Yet, one can easily notice that in research and education some 'arms' dominate and reshape others, leading to 'mimicry'. As such, some arms have stronger suckers than others have; some arms are more cunning than others are, better at camouflaging and imposing their power, such as 'American' multiculturalism, 'European' intercultural competence. In their article *Visualizing the knowledge domain of intercultural competence: A bibliometric analysis*, Peng et al. (2020) confirm the dominance of such voices in a particular sub-branch of intercultural scholarship. In recent years, I have noted that ideologies such as *intercultural mediation, citizenship,* but also *critical cultural awareness,* and *intercultural responsibility,* all from the 'West', have gained force in global scholarship and become at times mere 'speech acts' (Ahmed, 2006). Many other perspectives, their concepts, notions and methods are unheard of outside their context. For example, as we shall see the centrality of for example, 'economic development' in Chinese discourses of interculturality and the idea of 'cultural confidence' are 'alien' outside the Middle Kingdom.

To conclude about the *octopus* metaphor, I argue that it helps us become aware of the real complexity of the notion of interculturality while asking us to bear in mind our common global goals, whose meanings need to be renegotiated again and again. The metaphor can also support us in noticing genuinely global (i.e. diverse) ways of problematizing and offering solutions to issues of interculturality. By doing so, interculturality as an octopus can offer more knowledge about interculturality from around the world and thus contribute a little to 'epistemic justice', a way of tacking silent discrimination (Fricker, 2007; R'boul, 2020). The metaphor can also urge us to be motivated to be interested in other 'arms' and to look out for other solutions and ideas.

The detour via the metaphor of the octopus suggests that we focus more systematically on the following questions:

- How to give a voice to different 'arms' of interculturality as an octopus and enjoy more *plasticity*?
- How to gain 'discursive rights', the right to speak beyond intercultural 'common sense' pushed forward by the 'West'?
- How to learn *with* each other between and amongst the 'arms'?
- How to prepare to evaluate the characteristics of each 'arm' in terms of *ideology, language-thought, economic-political aspects*?

This all comes down to the aforementioned idea of *interculturalizing interculturality*. This book on Chinese stories of interculturality presents some answers to these questions while contributing more questions and answers—*ad infinitum*. Following the German physicist and satirist G. C. Lichtenberg (2012: 35): "One's first step in wisdom is to question everything—and one's last is to come to terms with everything."

On the Obligation to Listen to Other Stories of Interculturality

The previous section highlights an important component of working on interculturality globally: we need to listen to others and to ourselves. The composer Igor Stravinsky (in Walsh, 2007: 339) helps us make an important distinction between *to listen* and *to hear*: "To listen is an effort, and just to hear is no merit. A duck hears also." In his music, Stravinsky tried to disrupt the way we listen to music by creating polytonality, combining different types of notes of a specific chord. He actually organized rhythm and melody in his famous piece called the *Rite of Spring* (1913) following

1 INTRODUCTION: WHY 'CHINESE' STORIES OF INTERCULTURALITY?

a principle named *tolchok*, from Russian толчок which means *to push* and *hit*. By doing so, the composer asked his listeners to accept some form of dissonance, that is, the combination/superposition of tones that are 'pushing' their listening to his music in different directions.

I argue that working on interculturality requires employing a *tolchok* (толчок) technique, to be pushed and hit in all directions, to experience 'shock' while accepting exchange and change when acquainting oneself with and listening to other ways of 'doing' interculturality. Until now, Westernized ideologies have been upheld as the yardstick for 'anything intercultural' on the academic and education markets. Proposing to listen to 'Chinese stories of interculturality' represents толчок. Of course, like the circulating and dominating Western ideologies ('orders'), what China has to say about interculturality can also be labelled as *ideology*, since any assertion, positioning about the notion cannot but be ideological, embedded in economic-political perspectives. What we are asking is for our readers to listen to these stories before comparing, judging, fetishizing and condemning. There is a need to go beyond what Gu (2015) calls *sinologism*, an "alienated" Western-centric way of engaging and producing knowledge about China that distorts and presents negative, inferior, unbalanced images of the Middle Kingdom, its people and stories.

Two first Chinese elements, which we shall refer to as *discourse instruments* in the book, can help us problematize these issues further:

1. 邯郸学步 (Hándānxuébù) translates as *Handan Toddler; learning to walk in Handan; learning a style of walking* and is explicated by one of our students as follows: "This is an idiom that comes from an ancient anecdote. Once upon a time, in a place called Shouling (寿陵), there was a young man who heard that the people in another place named Handan (邯郸) can walk with great grace. He was so fascinated by it that he went to Handan to learn how to walk like them. In order to learn better, he forced himself to forget his original way of walking. When he finally arrived at Handan, he was excited, he sometimes learnt from the elders, sometimes from children and sometimes from women. But with such a method, he failed to grasp any of these walking postures. Since he had forgotten his original way of walking, he had to crawl back to his hometown. Now we use this idiom to describe a person who failed to copy others'

advantages while losing their own merits as a cost".[3] The same student draws the following conclusion about interculturality based on this discourse instrument: "In the context of interculturality, we should be cautious to such a situation as well. In communication, it is pleasant to discover good things in others and it is really helpful if we can learn from them properly. But we must always know who we are in these procedures." In other words, imitating others as far as discourses of interculturality are concerned, without being critical and reflexive about for example, the words, concepts and notions in different languages and English as an international language, we might lose ourselves in a form of interculturalspeak that makes very little sense in our own context. Having spoken to thousands of students and scholars around the world, I often have the impression that we are not talking about the same thing—or that we are not really talking to each other at all. Once, having given a keynote at a conference in Latvia, I was congratulated by a local professor for my 'interesting approach', which he had completely misunderstood—it could be because I was not clear in my explanations. Other 'stories' about the notion might thus be worth considering and listening to.

2. 百家争鸣 (Bǎijiāzhēngmíng), that is, contention of a hundred schools of thought. This refers to different schools of thought in the Warring States Period (770–476 BCE), such as Confucianism, Taoism, engaging in meaningful dialogues. This discourse instrument represents a more positive phenomenon since it suggests having the opportunity to express oneself freely, debating with each other. A student writes about 百家争鸣: "I believe this need for a free atmosphere also works in the context of intercultural communication. Every idea deserves to be heard and everyone should have the chance and the right to voice out their opinion if they want to. Speaking is an essential aspect of communication, while listening plays an important part as well. In such an environment, people may be effected to view things from a multi-angle perspective and ideas can mix and we can innovate more smoothly and faster".

---

[3] Quotes from students in English are verbatim in the book. We ask the reader to be tolerant towards the use of the English language in these quotes and to read them a couple of times to try to get a full sense of what the students try to express. Many a times they do use formulations and terms that may sound 'foreign' in English. Getting used to the depaysement of different Englishes in discourses of interculturality is essential for making interculturality more *intercultural*.

By engaging with ideas beyond the 'usual' and the 'accepted' we could allow, as Jullien (2016: 105) argues about the concept of the 'beautiful' from China, interculturality to "begin to emerge from its banality and even reveal a fascinating strangeness". Facing this novelty, we might enrich our views on self, other, the world, and what it means to be, meet and become with others.

CHINA HAS THE LANGUAGE TO SPEAK ABOUT INTERCULTURALITY, LET'S LISTEN TO HER TOO!

China has a very long history of interculturality (McCarthy et al., 2021; Dervin & Machart, 2017). Today, China experiences diversity, multifaceted forms of interculturality, but also hybridity and mélange, in ways which are much more complex than outsiders might ever imagine. A country with over 1 billion people, with many kinds of regions, cities, towns and villages, with 56 different Minzu groups, internal migrants moving from the countryside to megacities, international migrants from all over the world, access to international media, fiction, art, music, and so on. Chinese people do experience all kinds of interculturality on a daily basis. To get a 'small' sense of this complexity, let's listen to three Chinese students sharing their experiences of linguistic diversity, foods and eating habits in their country:

> Student 1: "When I had to catch a train at the end of a trip, I called a Didi [a Chinese ride-hailing company] driver. Because I was afraid of missing the train, the driver didn't come for a long time, so we didn't plan to call Didi, but the driver called me twice later to say that he had arrived. After getting on the car, we could not understand what the driver was saying due to poor language communication, but we knew that the driver took us to the railway station was not where we wanted to go. Maybe because I had located the destination incorrectly on my mobile phone, the navigation set on the driver's car kept showing that it deviated from the original route. The language communication was not smooth all the way, but fortunately the driver understood our meaning, adjusted the route and arrived in time without delaying the departure of the train. Get off when I was ready to pay, the driver said no, he said he made a mistake in the place, but also quickly drove away the car, he said: "nothing, nothing, no need not give [pay]", then I still paid the driver on the Didi app."
>
> Student 2: "(I was born and live in the south of China) When I eat something with my roommates who were born and live in the north, if we have

something different in eating habits, we may say it is cultural difference between the north and the south."

Student 3: "For example, when I'm eating with my roommates who are from the south of China, they put the rubbish (such as bones, or the food they don't like) on the plate, but I put the rubbish on the table. Then, we would say, "oh, you do that but I do this! This phenomenon is a cultural difference."

Student 4: "My roommate and I come from different parts of China. Recently we talked about preferred flavors in zongzi [food made of glutinous rice wrapped in bamboo] for different regions. Actually, northern people are more used to salty zongzi, while the southern part likes sweet ones more. So, I think regional distinctions on food are parts of different cultures, which is kind of hidden cultural influences on our daily life."

Language is also a complex issue in China, as we shall see throughout the book. Although most readers will know that the main language is called Mandarin, very few will be aware that people speak different dialects and languages in the Middle Kingdom—many are not mutually intelligible. On top of that, one could mention Chinese Sign Language (手语, literally: 'hand language'), spoken by around 20 million people in China, with many variants (Li et al., 2014).

A few words about the Chinese language are needed here since it will be used in the book. Chinese itself counts over 10,000 characters and from 50,000 to nearly 100,000 words. Characters are known as Hanzi (漢字) and derive from a long history, with many different styles and/or scripts (e.g. oracle bone inscriptions on the carapaces of tortoises during the *Shang* Dynasty, 1600–1046 BCE). Simplified characters (简体字, Jianti ji) started to be used as standardized Chinese characters in Mainland China in the 1950s. They are also used in Singapore while traditional characters are found in for example, Hong Kong and Macau. Characters were formed in different ways. Ideographics symbolize visualization of concepts through an iconic form. Pictographic characters use images as a basis (Arcodia & Basciano, 2021). Since the book is about humans coming together to 'do' interculturality, let me provide a few examples of different kinds of characters, including representations of human beings/ghosts, masks and headdresses in former versions of the characters:

- 異 (Yì): *strange, different, spooky*, is based on the representation of a dancer wearing a mask.
- 冀 (Jì): *to hope, to aspire, to wish*, is based on a dancer wearing a mask and horn ornaments.

- 每 (měi): *every, each*; remnant of a woman in headdress.
- 美 (měi): *beauty, beautiful*; represented originally a man in headdress, a chief of a tribe.
- 黑 (Hēi): *black, dark*; "The dots on the dancer's face stand for the tattoo. Tattooing the face was for fun, and had become a punishment in ancient China. The lower parts transformed into a fire-radical. Burns are often black" (Wang, 2018: 180).
- 鬼 (Guǐ): *ghost, spirit, apparition*; a figure with a mask and a tail ornament.
- 畏 (Wèi): *fear, respect*; a ghost dancing with a stick.

In the book we have collected about 50 *discourse instruments of interculturality*, which all derive from and compose what we call 'Chinese stories of interculturality'. I coined the idea of Chinese stories of interculturality as I became aware of the very specific discourse instruments that I kept coming across in China, on the streets, in books, newspapers, TV programmes, social media, and so on, and in discussions with my colleagues, friends and students. The discourse instruments include *aspects from indigenous philosophies, idioms, chengyu* (成语, that is, traditional Chinese idiomatic expressions composed of four characters), *two-part allegorical sayings* (歇后语, xiēhòuyǔ), *neologisms (a new word or phrase), slogans* and *mottos*, as well as *ideological elements* from the Communist Party of China. We treat all these discourse instruments of interculturality as 'folk theories', informing us of specific (but also at times similar) perspectives on the notion. The discourse instruments were selected by us, discussed, described, defined and translated together. When we felt we had reached saturation in terms of the topics covered, making sure we included as many diverse instruments as possible, we checked with each other their coherence and representativeness. We realize that more instruments could have been included in the book but, since this is the first book ever to focus on Chinese stories of interculturality, we feel that it is a stepping stone but urge others to continue this important work.

The book is aimed at Chinese and non-Chinese speakers, interested in enlarging their reflections and knowledge of interculturality, beyond the 'usual', 'imposed' and largely 'unchallenged' of today's scholarship and education on interculturality. The book does not require knowledge of Chinese and/or specialist information about China. In a similar vein, it is not a book for learning Chinese, although it stimulates interest and curiosity about the language as an important component of unthinking and rethinking interculturality. In fact, the book is intended to reflect with readers on 'Chinese stories of interculturality' and to support them to look in themselves as 'intercultural' beings, who are interested in the notion of interculturality. As such the book is meant to serve the purpose of mirroring: looking into the discourse instruments, on can reflect on oneself, the apparent 'otherness' of Chinese stories of interculturality helping us to do so. Writing about his provocative play *Ubu Roi*, Jarry's (1965: 83) comment about the exaggerating mirror fits well the purpose of this book:

> I intended that when the curtain went up the scene should confront the public like the exaggerating mirror in the stories of Madame Leprince de Beaumont, in which the depraved saw themselves with dragons' bodies, or bulls' horns, or whatever corresponded to their particular vice. It is not surprising that the public should have been aghast at the sight of its other self, which it had never before been shown completely.

The somewhat novel and—at times—destabilizing realm that the reader is about to enter is also meant to trigger some interest in noticing potential similarities between 'Chinese stories of interculturality' and other sets of stories. The reader will, in all likelihood, note *many* similarities with discourse instruments from other contexts—if not, we will urge them to do so throughout the book.

Let's turn to some of our students again to listen to what they have to say about how they see the 'Chinese stories of interculturality' that are at the centre of this book. These excerpts, written in English by the students, will already give an idea of the specific 'flavours' of these stories to our readers (see e.g. the use of phrases such as 'cultural integration', 'inner temperament', which might sound 'foreign' to our readers):

> (Student 1) "China is often seen as a monolith from foreign perspectives. However, heterogeneity and interculturality have kept characterizing China throughout its entire history. Chinese stories of interculturality actually represent the fusion of cultures, and form a new one as an entirety."
>
> (Student 2) "I think it may mean the encounters of different thinking methods, showing respect to each other, then learning from each other, and finally adding up some elements of other cultures to enrich Chinese culture. This process may be a bit long, sometimes not peaceful, and probably the elements taken in are overhauled by Chinese culture itself. For example, political power may play an important role in this changing process. If having a look at Wei Jin Southern and Northern Dynasties, the spreading of

1 INTRODUCTION: WHY '*CHINESE*' STORIES OF INTERCULTURALITY? 15

Buddhism was remolded by the authority, making it correspond with the official ideology."

(Student 3) "In my opinion, 'the Chinese story of interculturality' means how much China plays a role and how it affects the world within the context of interculturality. The concept of interculturality has a very far-reaching history in Chinese culture. During the Western Han Dynasty, Emperor Wu of the Han Dynasty sent Zhang Qian to the western regions. He traveled as far as Rome and North Africa, which greatly promoted cultural integration between the East and the West. Throughout Chinese history, there are countless stories about eminent monks' interculturality in spreading Buddhism. In the Tang Dynasty, Xuanzang traveled westward to Central Asia and even India to seek scriptures, whose story was later adapted into the famous novel *Journey to the West*. In addition, the story of Monk Jianzhen crossed the ocean six times to Japan to teach Buddhism also inspired generations in both China and Japan. Later in the Ming Dynasty, navigator Zheng He made seven voyages to the west, reaching as far as the east coast of Africa and the Red Sea. His career not only strengthened the exchange of Eastern and Western civilizations in the early 15th century, but also promoted peace and trade.

According to the above concepts, we can see that interculturality in ancient China meant spreading religious theories, opening up trade routes and an expanding tributary system. After the founding of the People's Republic of China, Premier Zhou Enlai went to Indonesia to attend the Asian-African Bandung Conference in 1955. Premier Zhou expressed China's position on the basis of the Five Principles of Peaceful Coexistence. This meeting produced the Ten Principles of Bandung Conference and the spirit of 'unity, friendship and cooperation'. This shows the official position of modern China on interculturality, which is mainly about respecting each other and non-interference".

(Student 4) "In my opinion, the Chinese story of interculturality means Chinese ways of engaging with interculturality which tend to be unknown or not so obvious and accessible for people from other parts of the world. These stories are of Chinese character and can show Chinese unique concern to the world and interculturality, and also can reflect Chinese inner temperament. At the spiritual level the Chinese story of interculturality mainly contains appeal for joint effort, the value of peace and sense of responsibility. At the implementation level, it contains Chinese cultural shows around the world, China's aid to countries and regions in need and active participation in international organizations."

In these quotes, students make references to China's history of interculturality and diversity, her role in today's world, as well as political and diplomatic efforts. The discourse instruments that we shall introduce, all find their origins in these 'stories'.

The aims of the book are manifold. First of all, it is not meant to provide 'definite' answers about interculturality as if China could help us solve all kinds of issues. The discourse instruments will help us ask questions about ourselves, others, who we are together, the world and most importantly, about how we see interculturality as an object of research and education. Some might mock the forms and contents of the instruments, arguing that they sound 'naïve', 'cheap philosophy', like 'sermons' and all kinds of negative comments that have been made about aspects of so-called Chinese wisdom (see Cheng, 2007).

Some might criticize the political tone of some discourse instruments, which often intertwin the present and the past, forgetting that many so-called Western theories are directly linked to (broader and dominating) political projects. Take as an example one of the most influential figures of interculturality in the world, Michael Byram, who has cooperated intensively with a political institution called the Council of Europe,[4] which has a clear agenda for Europe (and the world?). As such, in a 2022 book published in Byram's honour, *Intercultural Learning in Language Education and Beyond: Evolving Concepts, Perspectives and Practices* (edited by McConachry et al., 2022), a chapter written by a former employee of the Council of Europe, is entitled "Mike Byram's Commitment to Council of Europe Values"

This book is thus not about judging or deciding if the 'Chinese stories of interculturality' are 'right' or 'wrong' (or something else)—Western media have been doing this constantly since the beginning of the COVID-19 pandemic, condemning China for things that 'Western' countries themselves might have done/argued for in the past and might do and express today.[5]

For all these reasons, we ask the reader to approach the discourse instruments with an open mind, curiosity and thirst for renewed thinking about interculturality. Obviously, criticality and reflexivity are part of the complex processes of getting acquainted with the 'Chinese Stories of

---

[4] The Council of Europe was founded in 1949 and it includes 47 member-states. It is described as Europe's leading human rights organisation. This institution is not to be confused with the European Union. See https://www.coe.int/en/web/portal/

[5] As we shall see in the book, one of the Chinese discourse instruments of interculturality relates to unity and diversity. In the foreword to a document entitled *European Commission Guidelines for Inclusive Communication* from December 2021, Helena Dalli (EU Commissioner for Equality) makes use of the discourse instrument of 'United in Diversity' to justify what the document is about.

Interculturality'. However, 'cheap', 'unfair' and 'uninformed' judgements and condemnations have no place in intercultural work.

CHANGE AND EXCHANGE AS CONSTANTS IN CHINESE STORIES OF INTERCULTURALITY

As stated earlier, our book is not a 'Chinese' recipe book for interculturality. What it does bring to the reader is many opportunities to reflect on two terms that are central in interculturality: change and exchange. As such, as we shall see, the idea of *change* is omnipresent in many of the proposed discourse instruments. Change is also linked to the special times when this book was written (the COVID-19 pandemic) which has led to many changes—and more to come—and opened up our eyes to the kind of world that we had lived in, full of injustices, ignorance, petty attacks and discrimination, in societies at large, government initiatives, technology, and even education and academia. Keeping an eye on the changes to come, related to interculturality, will surely keep us busy for decades. Change is also here symbolic of what we can experience while looking into the mirror of the discourse instruments from this book.

One of our students summarize well the kind of change taking place in interculturality, using a Chinese discourse instrument, when asked "why can't we agree on a 'universal' and 'objective' model of intercultural competences?". She explains:

> The more I learn about interculturalism, the more I realise that it is not a 'certificate' that you can acquire through reaching any kind of standards, but more of an "气质" that cannot be defined simply."

气质 is composed of two characters for 1. vital energy and 2. quality-substance. For the student interculturality corresponds to qualities that change, evolve but also regress, in other words, to *vital energy*. The character 气 shows the vapours one can see when for example, rice is being cooked.

Change is also contained in the use of language to problematize interculturality in this book. For each discourse instrument, we have tried to propose several translations, knowing that they would not always make sense or be transparent for the reader. We urge you then to check the translations and to retranslate again and again for yourself and for others. Language matters here in the sense that it can help us (or not) communicate around 'Chinese stories of interculturality'. As hinted at earlier, many Chinese discourse instruments do not always make sense in English and deserve active retranslating and negotiating. With our students, we have looked into notions and terms such as *Cultural arrogance, culture convergence, self-segregation tendencies within cultures, mutual culture understanding and convergence.* It does take time to make sense of these English phrases, when translated directly from Chinese. Hence the need to translate words again and again with others, to try to find 'equivalents' that make sense even if it means using more or less words and operating transformations. If these words, phrases, sentences are not negotiated, someone will suffer and be potentially mistreated. For instance, they may not be taken seriously, considered as mere 'language massaging', looked down upon, trusted... And as the writer Nabokov (cited by Boyd, 2016: 421) put it, dictionaries are not always our friends here but our potential enemies.

Barbara Cassin (2016) talks about 'untranslatables' in her work, which she defines as "a symptom of difference between languages", suggesting that things should be translated again and again. She adds (ibid.: n.p.): "*ce qu'on ne cesse pas de (ne pas) traduire*: what never stops being (not) translated". In a similar vein, Eco (2001: 153) suggests that what matters in translation is not the denotation of words but their connotations. He provides the following example in Italian:

> the word *cool*, in English, denotes a physical state but in the idiom *keep cool* connotes a psychological one, so that a correct Italian translation should not be *rimani freddo* but rather *sta' calmo*.

One of our students, commenting on his perceived differentiated use of the word *culture* in China and Europe, asserts:

> European students (mainly my French friends) always use the word *culture* to describe a place or a country's art, music, literature and somethings like that. For example, they will use "rich culture" to describe countries like Russia and France for they produced many masterpieces. While, Asian students consider "culture" as customs. They like to say "culture difference" when they find different habits among students from different countries. Let's say, my Vietnamese roommate will say "Oh, it's culture difference" when I can't bear the smell of her favorite Vietnamese food. As for me, and maybe many other Chinese people, the word culture refers to something stable but which kept changing throughout history. We like to closely com-

1 INTRODUCTION: WHY 'CHINESE' STORIES OF INTERCULTURALITY? 19

bine traditional culture with our lifestyle today. In a word, I think the meaning of culture depends on how much a person is influenced by their own surroundings when they use it.

The reader will fully enjoy this book while reflecting on such aspects of language. At the same time, we suggest that they go beyond 纸上谈兵 (Zhǐshàngtánbīng, *talk on paper*), which means that someone only engages in *idle theorizing* but *not practicing*. Thinking about concrete examples while trying to make sense of the discourse instruments is a good practice for future engagement with interculturality but also for reflecting on past intercultural encounters. At the end of each chapter, we have added lists of further questions for you to reflect more on the content of the chapters. Answers to these questions may not be found straight after reading the chapters. That is why we recommend going back to the chapters and questions again and again, noting down one's answers each time and comparing them as we move further in our thinking. There are no right or wrong answers.

Finally, as a reminder, this book is not meant to be a Chinese language book and no knowledge of Chinese is required to make sense of it. In order to understand better and negotiate the meanings of the discourse instruments, we have used different kinds of resources and suggest that they are consulted by the readers for further references. These include:

- An online etymological dictionary of Chinese: https://www.purple-culture.net/chinese-english-dictionary/;
- The Etymonline.com website to check the etymology of some English words included in the book;
- The Key concepts in Chinese Thought and Culture website: https://www.chinesethought.cn/EN/.

We argue that unpacking and dissecting the characters in Chinese and reflecting on the etymology of the words in English can help us deepen our engagement with interculturality as an object of research and education. *To make interculturality more intercultural!*

The book is composed of the following chapters:

- Chapter 2—Approaching interculturality: Culture and civilization as discursive and reflexive tools, in which discussions of culture and identity; culture and identity as change and transformation; dis-

course instruments to analyse cultural phenomena and the use of *civilized* and *civilization* are reviewed.
- Chapter 3—Exploring and explaining experiences of interculturality contains presentations of tools to analyse interculturality from a macro-perspective and its potential consequences on the micro-perspective, discussions of understanding and explaining interculturality from a personal perspective.
- Chapter 4—'Doing' interculturality together: we introduce discourse instruments for positioning oneself towards intercultural encounters; working through the principle of harmony; making use of the continuum of difference and similarity; learning with each other; reciprocity in interculturality.
- Chapter 5—Making interculturality work together, as group/community members discusses Chinese political initiatives related to interculturality; reflecting on what togetherness entails within the context of Chinese Minzu; togetherness and interculturality from a more global perspective; the objectives and benefits of togetherness and learning about it.
- Chapter 6—Learning to 'do' interculturality: *Setting objectives for oneself* problematizes looking at the self; reflecting on 'doing' interculturality with the Other; practising complexity; plurality and modesty in reflexivity.
- Chapter 7—Pondering over language and interculturality shares discourse instruments related to the limits of language/misusing language; using language in interculturality; and qualifying language.
- Chapter 8 concludes the book by offering a summary as well as reflections on how to continue exploring stories of interculturality from around the world.

This book is a great example of our fruitful, honest and collegial cooperation globally. To our knowledge, this is the first of its kind, and we do hope that colleagues from around the world will benefit from our hard work, across two continents, trying to bring some fresh ideas and knowledge about a notion that matters deeply to us in global education. We do encourage others to follow our path and to 'dig into' alternative views and ideas about interculturality. This is the only way we can keep it meaningful and relevant for the decades to come.

Thinking Further

- After having read this introduction, reflect on what has already potentially surprised you and led you to unthink and rethink certain aspects of interculturality in global education. Are there elements in what I wrote that you disagree with?
- What metaphors can you think of to symbolize how you see interculturality at this stage? Can you explain why? In this introduction, I have included those of *the octopus* and *the telescope*.
- We shall see many examples of 'untranslatables' in the book. Can you already think of examples of such linguistic elements in discussions of interculturality in different languages?
- How do you understand Nabokov's argument that dictionaries are enemies not friends?
- Without trying to find information about them, what do you think the Chinese discourse instruments translated into English as *cultural arrogance, culture convergence, cultural confidence*, mean?
- Have you ever noticed that some people might understand and use the word culture in ways different from yours? Can you share some examples?
- I argue in this introduction—and throughout the book with my co-authors—that *change* and *exchange* are in fact the most important aspects of interculturality. We will come back to this point later. But, at this stage, what do you make of these two keywords?
- The idea of discourse instruments is central in the book. In the introduction, I provide the following categories: *aspects from indigenous philosophies, idioms, chengyu, two-part allegorical sayings, neologisms, slogans* and *mottos*, as well as *ideological elements*. You already have some knowledge about interculturality—we all do! Can you think of examples of such instruments in the languages you know that relate to different aspects of interculturality (e.g. expressing tolerance, respect)?

(continued)

(continued)

- This is how one of our students sees the importance of what they refer to as the role of the 'cultural industry' on interculturality: "I think worldwide advancement of cultural industry is of great benefit to the improvement of interculturality. By reading novels and comics, watching movies and TV dramas, listening to music, playing online games, and using worldwide apps or social networks, it is becoming easier and easier for the younger generation to get a taste of the lifestyles of different countries or regions, chat with friends from another corner of the globe, and see the larger world. Although the development of cultural industry may lead to problems such as unilateral cultural export, but when the whole world becomes more diverse, the problems arising in the process will be solved adequately". Do you share their optimistic view?
- Before moving on to the next chapter about culture and civilization, reflect on the idea of *making interculturality intercultural*. What does it mean to you at this stage?

References

Ahmed, S. (2006). The Nonperformativity of Antiracism. *Meridians, 7*(1), 104–126.

Aman, R. (2017). *Decolonising Intercultural Education: Colonial Differences, the Geopolitics of Knowledge, and Inter-epistemic Dialogue*. Routledge.

Arcodia, G. F., & Basciano, B. (2021). *Chinese Linguistics: An Introduction*. Oxford University Press.

Baker, W. (2021). From Intercultural to Transcultural Communication. *Language and Intercultural Communication*. https://doi.org/10.1080/14708477.2021.2001477

Boyd, B. (2016). *Vladimir Nabokov. The Russian Years*. Princeton University Press.

Cassin, B. (2016). Translation as Paradigm for Human Sciences. *Journal of Speculative Philosophy, 30*(3), 242–266.

Cheng, A. (2007). *Can China Think?* Seuil/College de France.

Dervin, F., & Jacobsson, A. (2021). *Teacher Education for Critical and Reflexive Interculturality*. Palgrave Macmillan.

Dervin, F., & Machart, R. (Eds.). (2017). *Intercultural Communication with China*. Springer.

Dervin, F., & Yuan, M. (2021). *Revitalizing Interculturality in Education. Chinese Minzu as a Companion*. Routledge.
Dervin, F., Yuan, M., Sude, & Chen, N. (2022). *Interculturality Between East and West. Unthink, Dialogue, and Rethink*. Springer.
Eco, U. (2001). *Experiences in Translation*. University of Toronto Press.
Ferri, G. (2018). *Intercultural Communication: Critical Approaches, Future Challenges*. Palgrave Macmillan.
Fricker, M. (2007). *Epistemic Injustice: Power and the Ethics of Knowing*. Oxford University Press.
Gu, M. D. (2015). *Sinologism. An Alternative to Orientalism and Postcolonialism*. Routledge.
Hugo, V. (1866). *The Toilers of the Sea*. Walter Scott Limited.
Ibelema, M. (2021). *Cultural Chauvinism: Intercultural Communication and the Politics of Superiority*. Routledge.
Ingoglia, S., Barrett, M., Iannello, N. M., Inguglia, C., Liga, F., Lo Cricchio, M. G., Tenenbaum, H., Wiium, N., & Lo Coco, A. (2021). Promoting Democratic and Intercultural Competences in the Primary School Context: The Experience of "Children's Voices for a New Human Space". *Journal of Clinical and Developmental Psychology, 3*(1), 45–57.
Jarry, A. (1965). *Selected Works*. Grove Press.
Jullien, F. (2016). *This Strange Idea of The Beautiful*. Seagull Books.
Kulich, S. J., Weng, L., Tong, R., & DuBois, G. (2020). Interdisciplinary History of Intercultural Communication Studies. In D. Landis & D. P. S. Bhawuk (Eds.), *The Cambridge Handbook of Intercultural Training* (pp. 60–163). Cambridge University Press.
Li, J., Yin, B., Wang, L., & Kong, D. (2014). Chinese Sign Language Animation Generation Considering Context. *Multimedia Tools and Applications, 71*, 469–483.
Lichtenberg, G. C. (2012). *Philosophical Writings*. State University of New York Press.
Mather, J. (2019). What Is in an Octopus's Mind? *Animal Sentience, 26*(1), 1–29.
McCarthy, G., Sun, Y., & Song, X. (2021). *Transcultural Connections: Australia and China*. Springer.
McConachy, T., Golubeva, I., & Wagner, M. (2022). *Intercultural Learning in Language Education and Beyond: Evolving Concepts, Perspectives and Practices*. Multilingual Matters.
Norman, M. D., Finn, J., & Tregenza, T. (2001). Dynamic Mimicry in an Indo-Malayan Octopus. *Proceedings of the Royal Society of London Series B, 268*, 1755–1758.
Peng, R.-Z., Zhu, C., & Wu, W.-P. (2020). Visualizing the Knowledge Domain of Intercultural Competence Research: A Bibliometric Analysis. *International Journal of Intercultural Relations, 74*, 58–68.

R'boul, H. (2020). Researching the Intercultural: Solid/Liquid Interculturality in Moroccan-Themed Scholarship. *The Journal of North African Studies*. Advance online publication.

Smith, G. (2021). *Other Minds: The Octopus and the Evolution of Intelligent Life*. William Collins.

Walsh, S. (2007). *Stravinsky – The Second Exile: France and America*. Pimlico.

Wang, H. (2018). *The Origins of Chinese Characters*. Beijing: Sinolingua.

Yuan, M., Sude, Wang, T., Zhang, W., Chen, N., Simpson, A., & Dervin, F. (2020). Chinese Minzu Education in Higher Education: An Inspiration for 'Western' Diversity Education? *British Journal of Educational Studies*, 68(4), 461–486.

CHAPTER 2

Approaching Interculturality: Culture and Civilization as Discursive and Reflexive Tools

INTRODUCTION

The keywords of *culture* and *civilization* have been central in understanding ourselves and the way we interact with people from other parts of the world since the eighteenth century, when European Modernity emerged and 'forced' us to think about these elements through these multifaceted and polysemic concepts (Eriksen, 2001; Chemla & Fox Keller, 2017). Although critiques have been addressed at the concepts in the human and social sciences, they are still strong globally in research, education and on a daily basis (Dervin & Jacobsson, 2021). Civilization, however, is less common than culture in most European countries and tends to be limited to the space of museums, history books and in the phrase *the clash of civilisations* which was popularized by Huntington (2002). In China today, the two words appear to be omnipresent, especially in public spaces where they are used in many and varied ways, and at times, as synonyms (see Fig. 2.1).

In this chapter, it is not our intention to try to define the words culture and civilization in Chinese or English (see e.g. Han, 2019; Gaukroger, 2020). These two concepts have been discussed umpteen times and defined in hundreds of different ways (see Fang, 2019). What we are

© The Author(s), under exclusive license to Springer Nature Switzerland AG 2022
M. Yuan et al., *Change and Exchange in Global Education*, Palgrave Studies on Chinese Education in a Global Perspective, https://doi.org/10.1007/978-3-031-12770-0_2

Fig. 2.1 A banner with the word civilization in Chinese being displayed on the streets of Beijing

interested in here is how they are used in the discourse instruments that we have collected, not so much to learn about what they mean—we repeat: *they are polysemic in Chinese too!*—but to see how they are used, for what purposes and, most importantly, how they might help us unthink and rethink our engagement with interculturality.

Let us start with etymological considerations for the two English words. Culture is from Latin *cultura* for *agriculture, cultivating*. In the sixteenth century, the word started to be used to refer to getting educated and intellectually refined. It is not until the late nineteenth century that the word culture was used to mean collective customs and achievements of a people. This last meaning tends to dominate today, although it is unclear as to what it includes and excludes, and what are the boundaries between 'collectives'. Finally, we note that the popular idea of *culture shock* in intercultural research dates back to the 1940s.

Civilization used to refer to a law which makes a criminal process civil and shifted to *civilized condition of people*, which is attested from the end of the eighteenth century. The sense of a particular human society in a civilized condition is from the early nineteenth century. If used today, the concept tends to refers to the latter. The word comes from Latin *civilis* which means *relating to a citizen, relating to public life*, but also *popular, affable, courteous*. The word has a link to the word for *city* too.

Now let's look at the Chinese words for culture and civilization, which will be at the centre of our discussions of the first set of discourse instruments to follow. We note that in Chinese the two words can sometimes be used as mere synonyms. The two words share a similar first character: 文 (wén), which by itself, can refer to different elements such as *language, culture*, and *writing*. Its pictographic is a tattooed chest, representing writing. This character is also used in the words for *literature* and *art* in the Chinese language.

Culture translates as 文化 (wén huà) (see Fig. 2.2). The second character of culture is 化 and is composed of two sub-characters, one for *man*,

Fig. 2.2 The word *culture* in Chinese and English used on a banner to promote sports at Minzu University of China

Fig. 2.3 The word *culture* in Chinese in a bookstore

person/people and another for *spoon, ladle/knife*. Huà means to *make into, to change into,* and indicates *-ization* in English. It is found in many words reflecting change such as variation, modernization, intensification and so on. The word culture in Chinese used to refer to "a situation wherein a change takes place for one side or both sides concerned, as a result of their contact with each other" (Fang, 2019: 9). 化 shows a man straight up and one man upside down. The very word 文化 (wén huà) also refers to *educated* (see Fig. 2.3). 没文化 (méi wén huà) is *uneducated, lacking education*. 没 means *no*.

明 (míng) composes the second character of *civilization*. By itself it means *bright, clear*, but also *to understand*. Its ideographic is based on the light of the sun 日 and moon 月. This seems to correspond to the idea that civilization is meant to 'bring light' to those who embrace it. In Chinese, civilization refers to human inventions, creations and spirit and hints at the idea of moving away from what could be considered as 'barbarism'.

This chapter is based on the following sections: Culture and Identity, Culture and Identity as Change and Transformation, Discourse Instruments to Analyse Cultural Phenomena, Use of Civilized/Civilization and Miscellaneous.

Culture and Identity

This first set of discourse instruments is based on the interrelations between the idea of culture and identity—another central concept in interculturality (Dervin & Risager, 2017). The way we include culture in discussions and reflections around the notion can both help us reflect on who we are with others (and vice versa) and what interculturality can 'do' to identity.

文化自觉—*Wén huà zì jué*
Can be translated as: *Cultural self-awareness*.

自觉 translates as *conscious* and *aware* and is composed of:

- 自 (zì, *self, oneself*), with a pictographic of a nose (pointing at one's nose to refer to self). The character is also contained in the words for *freedom* and *liberty*, as well as *nature/natural* in Chinese.
- 觉 (jué) is composed of sub-characters for *cover* and *to see, to observe* and *to meet*. The word can mean *to feel, to find that* and *thinking/aware*.

The idea of *cultural self-awareness* was proposed by the Chinese sociologist Fei Xiaotong, famous for his work on rural China and Chinese Minzu (see Fei, 2015). With this discourse instrument, Fei wished to urge people to be aware of their own 'cultural roots', to understand what culture is about, to become self-confident and to reflect on the consequences of economic development on culture and identity. For Fei, if people are ready to show open-mindedness and understanding, this could lead to (global) harmony and cooperation in development (ibid.). In other words, the more I can reflect on my own culture and civilization, the more I can open up to others.

In English, the idea of awareness was formulated earlier as *awaredom*. Aware is from late Old English *gewær* which meant *watchful, vigilant*.

In order to develop cultural self-awareness, one needs to 'watch' oneself and others, to reflect on our own specificities and our place in the global world, while pondering over the impact of economic-political forces on how we think about who we are and what other people represent for us and for themselves.

文化翻译—*Wén huà fān yì*
Can be translated as: *Cultural translation, cultural awareness*.

翻 (fān) stands for *to translate, to interpret, to decode* but also *to cross*. The character for wings 羽 contained in the full character translates as *wings* and gives the meaning to the character. 译 (yì) can also mean *to translate* and *to interpret* and contains the sub-character for *words* and *speech* (讠, yán). Cultural translation refers to the process of 'passing on' elements from a given translation, while demonstrating awareness of target and original cultures. Being able to explain the differences between the translated work and the original is also part of the skill to translate culture.

In the English language, the verb *to translate* originally referred to removing from one place to another, from Latin *translatus*—carried over, across, beyond. The idea of crossing is contained in the origins of the words for translation in both Chinese and English. Translating is crossing over from and to another language, and back. Eco's (2001) suggestion that translation should be 'world-for-world' rather than merely 'word-for-word' suggests a similar idea as 文化翻译.

文化素质—*Wén huà sù zhì*

Can be translated as: *Cultural/inner quality, cultural competence, education.*

The character 素 (sù) is translated as *raw silk, white, plain*, but also *essence* and *the nature of something* or *someone*. Its ideographic is that of a silken thread hanging off a tree. 质 (zhì) is equivalent to the English for *character, nature, quality*. The character is formed by means of the sub-character for *cliff, building on top*, the sub-character for *ten, complete* and that of *sea shell, money* and *currency* (which conveys the meaning of the character).

Cultural/inner quality refers to people's capacities, moral strengths and abilities to engage in and complete a certain activity. It also refers to people having a good knowledge of the human and social sciences, as demonstrated in their writing and dialoguing around ideas with and for others. One could argue that 文化素质 is very relevant for reflecting on intercultural encounters.

文化修养—*Wén huà xiū yǎng*

Can be translated as: *Cultural cultivation, accomplishment* or even *self-cultivation.*

修 (xiū) is another polysemic word, from *dried meat, a private teacher's fee, to decorate, to embellish, to repair, to build, to cultivate* and so on. The character is composed of sub-characters for *distant, far* and *hair/sunlight*, which gives the word its meaning. 修 is also found in words such as *to build, to revise*. The fourth character 养 (yang) translates as *to raise (animals), to bring up (children), to support* and *to give birth*. Its pictophonetic is based on characters for *a sheep goat* and *son, child*, which conveys its meaning.

To cultivate here refers to understanding, absorbing and learning elements, for example, from the human, social and technological sciences with a view to improve and, especially, complexify the way one sees the world. The English word *cultivation* is from Latin *cultivare* meaning *to plough, to rake*. 文化修养 could entail being acquainted with and knowledgeable about ideas from different parts of the world so that one can have a balanced view of the world—to step outside one sphere of explaining and understanding.

文化主体性— *Wén huà zhǔ tǐ xìng*

Can be translated as: *Cultural subjectivity*.

主体性 translates as subjectivity. 主 (zhǔ) is *the owner, the master* or *the host* and can also refer to *God* and *the Lord*. Its pictographic is that of a lamp 王 with a flame ヽ. The character is found in words for *main, principal, a director, a chairperson, socialism* and *democracy*. In any case, 主 indicates that one is in control. 体 (tǐ) means *the body, form, style, substance* (amongst others) and has the radical for *a person* (亻, rén) and *root, origin*. Finally, 性 (xìng) can be translated as *nature, character, quality, attribute* but also *gender* and correspond to *-ity* or *-ness* in the English language. The meaning of the character is indicated by the sub-character for *heart*. Another sub-character for *life, birth* and *growth* also composes 性. The Chinese word for *personality* also contains this character.

In English *subjectivity* is from Latin *subiectus* which means *lying under, below, near bordering on* and, allegorically, *subjected, subdued*. Subjectivity as personal and idiosyncratic is from the end of the eighteenth century, before that, the notion referred to submissiveness and obedience.

Cultural subjectivity here refers to the capacity of social beings to reflect on their perceptions of their and other people's culture, especially in relation to belonging and identity. The notion also hints at the need for people to open up to other 'cultural elements' and to not just build confidence solely about their own. As the first character of subjectivity, 主, hints at, it is about becoming both the 'owner' and the 'host' of cultural elements.

文化基因— *Wén huà jī yīn*
Can be translated as: *Cultural gene.*

基 (jī) can be translated as *base* and *foundation* in English. It is composed of two sub-characters for *his, her, its, their* and *soil, earth, items made of earth*, with the latter conveying the meaning of 基. 因 (yīn) means *cause* and *reason* and represents *an enclosure/a border* containing *big, great, vast, deep*. Gene is thus the *cause* and *reason* for *who we are*, for our *identity*.

Cultural genes is a metaphorical concept used to refer to elements such as beliefs, habits, values that are passed onto us and acquired, actively or passively, consciously or unintentionally. Although they can appear to be 'inherited', these elements have and can (be) change(d) with time, space, encounters, mixing, juxtaposing and at times by protecting them. The idea of 'cultural heritage' could pass as a synonym for *cultural gene*.

文化常识— *Wén huà cháng shí*
Can be translated as: *Cultural commonsense, cultural literacy, cultural knowledge* and *Chinese culture.*

常识 means *common sense* and *general knowledge* in English. 常 (cháng) translates as *always and often* but also *common* and *general*. One of the sub-characters is used for the words for a *cloth, curtain, a handkerchief* or *a towel*. 识 (shí), containing the sub-character for *speech, ways*, that conveys the meaning, implies *to know* and *knowledge*. It is found in words such as *consciousness, awareness* and *ideology* in Chinese.

文化常识 thus refers to the kind of basic knowledge that one should/could master about a given culture, one's own included (see Fig. 2.4). 文化常识 often has to do with knowledge about Ancient China. In the famous Chinese end of secondary education exams, the Gaokao and civil service examinations, such basic knowledge is often tested. This includes but is not limited to in the Chinese context: knowledge about solar terms, history, geography, ancient music and so on. The French idea of 'culture générale' shares the same idea as this Chinese discourse instrument.

文化归属感— *Wén huà guī shǔ gǎn*
Can be translated as: *A cultural (sense of) belonging.*

Fig. 2.4 Book entitled 中国历史常识 ('general knowledge of Chinese literature') by Zheng Zhenduo (2019), published by Tiandi Press

归属感 could translate as a sense of belonging, especially in trying to foster it. 归 (guī) means *to return, to go/give back to, to be taken care of by, to belong to, to gather together* and has an ideographic of a wife 帚 returning home. 属 is composed of sub-characters for body, corpse and the name of a dynasty founder (禹, yǔ). It can mean *category, family members, to belong to*, or simply: *to be*. And the last character 感 (gǎn) translates as *to feel, to move, to affect*. Its ideographic is that of two hearts beating together. The character is found in Chinese words for gratitude, emotion, feelings between two people.

In English, the verb *to belong* is from Old English *langian*, which means *to pertain to* and *to go along with*.

文化归属感 is about identifying with, feeling a special connection and bond with a given culture, which creates a sense of community and togetherness with other group members. A single person can experience a sense of cultural belonging with multiple collectivities. Moderation and modesty in 文化归属感 can help opening up to the other.

Culture and Identity as Change and Transformation

Change and transformation have been keywords used constantly in the past to problematize the meaning of life, sociality and the human. For example, one fragment from the Greek philosopher Heraclitus (540–480 BCE) reads, "Το μόνο πράγμα που είναι σταθερό είναι η αλλαγή" (*The only thing that is constant is change*). A Chinese discourse instrument says the same: 宇宙间一切事物都是不断演变的 (Yǔzhòu jiān yíqiè shìwù dōu shì búduàn yǎnbiàn de), *Everything in the universe changes constantly*. As a reminder, *-ality* in interculturality hints at a never-ending process of negotiating the *inter-* between those involved in interculturality.

动静—*Dòng jìng*
Can be translated as: *Sign of activity, movement and stillness.*

动 (dòng) means *to move, to set in motion*, but also *to change*. The character is subdivided into a character for *cloud, to say* and *speak* and another one for *strength, power, capability*. The character composes words that have to do with to *exercise (sports), physical labour*, amongst others. 静 (jìng) means *quiet, calm* and refers to *a lack of movement*. It is subdivided into a character for *nature's colours, blue, green* and *black* and another for *to dispute, to fight, to contend*.

The discourse instrument, which is based on the dissonance between stillness and movement, comes from the *Book of Changes* or the *I Ching*—a book of oracles dating back thousands of years. The opposed poles of stillness and movement arranged in a continuum summarize well the way elements such as culture, civilization and identity function: things are co-(re-)(de-) constructed with the people we meet, while at the same time they might hold back against change for a while. Meeting someone interculturally always involves this never-ending process of 动静: while we get to know each other, discuss, dis-/agree, do things together, we pull ourselves and the other in different directions on the continuum of stillness and movement. For example, we might stereotype ourselves ("we Germans are xxx"—a form of stillness) while questioning in the same sentence this very same stereotype and thus including movement ("But as a German I am not xxx"). Fred has referred to this phenomenon as *Janusian* (Dervin, 2016), in reference to the double-faced God Janus.

变化—*Biàn huà*
Can be translated as: *Variety, change.*

This discourse instrument is based on a somewhat tautological combination of characters. 变 (Biàn) means *to change, to transform* and *to become different* and is constructed by means of a sub-character for *also, too* and another character for *and, again* and *in addition.* 化 is the same character as in the Chinese word for culture, which we have seen repeatedly. It also indicates change.

The word change in English is from old French for *exchange, reward, reciprocation.* The phrase *to change (one's) mind* is from 1590s.

The idea of the discourse instrument 变化 is that only through constant change can we permanently exist and develop. Interculturality must help us open our eyes to transformations and accept that change is part of our co-existence, co-construction of who we are when we are together. Only through change can we start doing interculturality together.

发展—*Fā zhǎn*
Can be translated as: *Development, progress, change.*

发展 translates as 'becoming different' and contains the characters for 'hair' and 'to spread out' (发) as well as 'show'/exhibition (展). The ideographic of zhǎn is laying out clothes for sale in a market.

In English *development* comes from French for *to unroll, to unfold.*

The word 发展, especially economic advancement, is often used in conjunction with ensuring that different kinds of people and regions reap the benefits of modernization. Development also goes hand in hand with interculturality since the services, goods and people taking part in economic activities can cooperate and contribute together to better situations for individuals. This important aspect is often camouflaged in global research on interculturality under labels such as, for example, social justice and equality. Although the idea of 发展 might sound a bit too blunt in some contexts, it reminds us to bear in mind the somewhat uncomfortable idea that capitals do matter in intercultural relations—for better or worse.

提高全民文明素质、文化素质—*Tí gāo quán mín wén míng sù zhì, wén huà sù zhì*

Can be translated as: *Improve education on culture, civility and arts* (word-for-word: *Improve the civilized and cultural qualities of all people*).

This discourse instrument goes hand in hand with the previous one but from a more humanistic way.

全民 means *whole people, all people*. 全 (quán) refers to *all, whole, every* and has an ideographic of jade put away for safe-keeping. 民 (mín) is a common word in China to refer to *people*, but also to *nationality* and *a citizen*. Its ideographic depicts an eye pierced by a dagger, which is an old mark of slavery. 民 is also contained in the words for *peasant, democracy* and *resident/inhabitant*—and in *minzu*, the word used to refer to different 'ethnic' groups in China.

素质 is the word for *quality*, and is composed of 素 (sù) for *raw silk, white, plain*, with an ideographic of a silken thread hanging off a tree. 质 (zhì) translates as *character, nature*, and *quality*, with the sub-character for *sea shell, money*, and *currency* conveying its meaning.

What improving "the civilized and cultural qualities of all people" means can take on different forms around the world. The quality of such endeavours can be judged based on how one defines 'civilized'—which, for example, in the Chinese context can range from politeness to technologically advanced—and 'cultural'—which in a given context might refer to education, literacy and so on. When one sees these words, one always needs to interrogate systematically the context where they are uttered and used to problematize their meanings and connotations. The discourse instrument urges us to rethink the issue of power of decision for change.

改造落后的文化—*Gǎi zào luò hòu de wén huà*

Can be translated as: *To transform a backward culture.*

改造 means *to transform, to remodel*; 落后 *to fall behind, to lag*, for example in technology. 改 (Gǎi) is *to change, to alter* and *to transform*, with an ideographic of a hand with a stick disciplining a kneeling child. 造 (zào) can be translated as *to make, to build, to manufacture*, and is composed of sub-characters for *to walk* and *to tell, inform*. 落 (luò) is about *retrogressing, declining*, based on sub-characters for *grass, plant, herb* and *a city*. Finally, 后 (hòu) refers to *an empress, queen, ruler* but also *behind, rear* and *later*. Its ideograph is that of a person leaning forward to orders from a person's mouth.

The straightforward idea of 'backward culture' might sound provocative and controversial to some readers. It has been part of some discourse instruments to describe *superstition, ignorance*, and *vulgarity* in culture, and how, by discarding some of these elements, one might become more 'cultured', more 'civilized'. In Chinese, there is often also an indication of economic development as an outcome of this process. What the three terms superstition, ignorance and vulgarity mean in different languages, different times and spaces, needs to be discussed, problematized and re-negotiated. Nothing is any of these from the outset and might depend on ideological beliefs. Therefore, what is considered as 'backward culture' always needs to be considered in relation to the following questions: who uses the instrument and for whom? Why do they consider something as 'backward culture' and how do they justify their opinion? What does calling something 'backward' as culture tell us about the one who uses the discourse instrument? What do the suggestions for change tell us about the utterer's ideologies and (short- and long-term) objectives as well as their relation with the ones targeted as having a 'backward culture'?

Discourse Instruments to Analyse Cultural Phenomena

人文交流—*Rén wén jiāo liú*

Can be translated as: *cultural and people-to-people exchange*.

人文 refers to *the humanities, human affairs* and even *culture*; 交流 *to exchange, interaction* and *social contacts*.

交 (jiāo) is *to hand over, to deliver, to pay money* (amongst others), with an ideographic of a person with crossed legs. The character is found in words expressing *transportation, exchange, to hand over*. 流 (liú) refers to the ideas of *flowing, circulating*, or *a stream of water*. It contains the sub-character for *water* and *uncultivated*.

In English, the word *exchange* is from Latin *excambium*, *ex-* meaning *out* and *cambire trade, negotiate*.

This discourse instrument suggests that, through communication, people can exchange ideas, feelings, 'interculturally' and start to flow, circulate like water—ideally benefitting each other.

文化词汇—*Wén huà cí huì*
Can be translated as: *Culture-loaded words/cultural vocabulary.*

词汇 means *a word* but also *vocabulary*. 词 (cí) refers to *a word, statement, speech* and is based on sub-characters for *words, to speak* and *to take charge of, to control*. 汇 (huì) is *to remit, to exchange*, and has an ideographic of *water collected in a container.*

This discourse instrument refers to words, vocabulary produced in specific places, regions and countries. These can emerge from individuals, the business world, decision-making, cultural productions such as films, social media and so on. For example, in French, the word 'le bins', which means *mess*, was first used in a very popular film released in the 1990s and spread to common language. Many neologisms (new words) are created in such a way today (see Fig. 2.5).

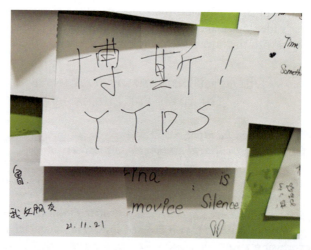

Fig. 2.5 An example of 文化词汇: *YYDS* in Chinese stands for 永远的神 (Yǒngyuǎn de shén), an expression used to show great admiration for someone and translates as *eternal/forever God*. YYDS are the first letters of each word from the Pinyin of 永远的神

文化底蕴—Wén huà dǐ yùn
Can be translated as: *Cultural deposits, cultural heritage.*

底蕴 means *inside information* or *concrete details*. 底 (dǐ) translates as *background, bottom, base* and revolves around sub-characters for *broad, wide* and the name of an ancient Chinese tribe (dǐ). 蕴 (yùn) means *to accumulate, to hold in store, to contain*, with sub-characters for *grass, weed, plant* and *vague/confused*.

This discourse instrument is equivalent somehow to the idea of cultural heritage, which can be defined as unique characteristics such as values and worldviews held by groups of people. Architecture can also be considered as 文化底蕴. The word *deposits*, which is often used in geology to refer to sedimentary beds, hints at the foundations of cultural elements in a given place and time.

Finally, *heritage* in English comes from Latin *heres* for *heir*. The current meaning of the word (passed down from ancestors) dates back to the early seventeenth century.

文化创新—Wén huà chuàng xīn
Can be translated as: *Cultural innovation.*

The characters 创新 (chuàng xīn) mean *to bring forth new ideas* (i.e. innovation). 创 is subdivided into a character for *cabin, barn* and *knife* (which gives the word innovation its meaning in Chinese). It refers to *beginning, starting, creating*. 新 (xīn) refers to *new/newly* and is found in for example the name of the Chinese autonomous region of Xinjiang (literally: *the new frontier*). Its ideographic is a freshly chopped tree. Innovation in Chinese is thus a new beginning, creating anew.

Innovation in English is from Latin *innovationem* which means *to change, to renew*.

In China, the idea of cultural development (often intertwined with economic development) relates to cultural innovation, which includes for example, the creation of specific practices and the invention of new technologies (in a broad sense). Interculturality also involves innovation since the encounter of two entities (individuals, cultural elements and artefacts) must lead to 'joint inventions' should the encounter be successful. This requires balancing between what each considers as 'acceptably changeable' on both sides and refusing change to innovate. Honest dialogue, whereby each contemplates multiple facets of change and viewpoints, must thus take place.

文化本土化—*Wén huà běn tǔ huà*
Can be translated as: *Cultural localization*.

本土化 is *to localize* and contains the following characters:

- 本 (běn) for *root, origin, source*, with an ideographic of a tree with its roots highlighted;
- 土 (tǔ) for *earth, dust, clay* but also *local* and *indigenous*, whose pictographic is a lump of clay on a potter's wheel—the character is used in the Chinese words for *territory, country, climate*.

化 is still the character that we have encountered many times (and many times to come), which refers *to change*.

In English, the word *local* is from Latin *locus*, meaning *a place, spot*.

文化本土化 calls for specific systems of thoughts (beliefs, habits, symbols) to be retained and safeguarded for example, modernizing and the introduction of external elements into a given geopolitical space. It is thus some form of cultural awareness within today's accelerated globalization/change (Eriksen, 2016), where some global dominating cultural elements and beliefs might overshadow local practices. Again, balancing global and local elements in the various societies that compose our world should be a priority in interculturality.

文化建设—*Wén huà jiàn shè*
Can be translated as: *Cultural construction*.

建设 means *to build, to construct*. 建 (jiàn) refers to *founding, setting up, constructing* and is based on a sub-character of *the writing brush, pencil*. The second character 设 (shè) is about *arranging, founding, displaying* (with one of the sub-characters indicating the use of a tool/a weapon).

In English, the word *construction* is from Latin: *com, with, together* and *struere* for *to pile up, to erect*.

文化建设 is represented by the many and varied cultural creations in fields such as sports, literature, art, and even science. The discourse instrument also hints at the use of scientific and technological innovation for educating people to explain and understand tomorrow's world.

文化强国—*Wén huà qiáng guó*
Can be translated as: *A culturally strong country*.

强国 also translates as *cultural power*. 强 can mean *strong, powerful, better, vigorous* and is composed of a sub-character for *a bow* (curved, arched). 国 is the word for *country, nation* and *state*. Its ideographic is that of a treasure within a country's borders. It is found in the very name of China 中国 (zhōng guó).

A culturally strong country is both confident about its distinctive 'identity' and 'culture' while being flexible enough to cooperate and learn with other countries. Like most countries having done some form of 'nation branding' (Freire, 2021), this discourse instrument is part of the Chinese national strategic policy.

文化输出—*Wén huà shū chū*
Can be translated as: *Cultural output*.

输出 means *to export, to output* and is composed of:

- 输 for *to lose, to transport, to enter* (e.g. a password). The word is based on the sub-characters for *a cart, a vehicle* and *to consent, to approve*.
- 出 for *to go out, to occur, to produce*. It has an ideographic of a sprout growing out of a container.

文化输出 is to present, introduce and promote one's own culture to outsiders. Interculturally, it is always difficult to balance such acts between modesty and arrogance. Essentialism might also appear when presenting one's culture. It is thus necessary to be realistic and honest about who we are (as a member of a given culture), to present 'good' and 'challenging' aspects and to leave the door opened to explore similitudes between 'us' and 'them'.

文化复兴—*Wén huà fù xīng*
Can be translated as: *Cultural renaissance, revival*.

复兴 means *to revive* and *to rejuvenate*. Its first character is 复 which can translate as *to repeat, to overlap, to restore*. Its ideographic is that of a person who goes somewhere every day. The character is found in words such as the adjective *complex* in Chinese. 兴 is composed of two sub-characters, one for *one, a/an* and *alone*, and another for *eight, all around* and *all sides*.

In English *to rejuvenate* is from Latin for *young again*. *To revive* is directly from Latin *reviver, to live again*.

文化复兴, cultural revival and renaissance, aims to offer guidelines for building up awareness of and the development of (here) Chinese traditional culture in relation to today's global conditions.

文化折扣—*Wén huà zhé kòu*
Can be translated as: *Cultural discount.*

折 (zhé) has an ideographic of a hand wielding an axe. In English, it means *to fold, to break, to turn*. 扣 (kòu) translates as *to fasten, to button, discount, to cover*. The word is based on sub-characters for *hand* and *mouth/entrance/gate*.

Discount in English is from the early seventeenth century word meaning "abatement", based on Mediaeval Latin *discomputus*.

文化折扣 refers to cultural elements being somewhat 'downgraded', sometimes looked down upon and/or totally ignored internationally due to a lack of recognition and understanding in other parts of the world. This phenomenon can derive from economic, political, ideological, financial but also linguistic reasons. A lack of curiosity, biases and stereotypes but also unequal power relations between 'us' and 'them' can lead to 'cultural discount'.

文化污染—*Wén huà wū rǎn*
Can be translated as: *Cultural pollution, Unhealthy spiritual and cultural products.*

污染 means *pollution, contamination*. 污 is the character for *dirty, filthy, corrupt*. *Water* and *to lose, fail* compose the character. 染 refers to *dyeing, acquiring, contaminating* and has an ideographic of water and wine mixed in a wooden bowl. The character is found in Chinese words such as an *infectious disease, epidemic*.

In English, *pollution* is from Latin *polluere, to soil, defile, contaminate*. The idea of *a contaminated environment* is noted from 1860.

Cultural pollution is a potentially controversial term in the English language and it should be considered carefully and reflexively. In the Chinese context, this concept refers to spiritual and cultural elements that can be considered troubling, illegal and morally questionable (e.g. pornography, some forms of superstition, violence). In order to deal with different aspects of 'cultural pollution', laws and regulations in different countries or globally have been made available. When considering this discourse instrument, let us not condemn it too quickly but reflect on why it exists and if and how similar elements might be available in our own contexts, but formulated in a different way. We must remember that the use of the word 'culture' in the Chinese version could refer to different things and phenomena.

Use of Civilized/Civilization

In this set of discourse instruments, we have collected slogans, mottos that we have noted in public and/or tourist places in China. As the reader will notice, the use of the words *civilized/civilization* is omnipresent in such contexts. Although the two words appear in the proposed translations below, in the English language, alternatives could be used such as *no* as in '*no polluting*'.

旅游美时美刻，文明随时随地—*Lǚ yóu měi shí měi kè, wén míng suí shí suí dì*
Can be translated as: *Behave politely on vacation, civilization will show; (word-for-word) Travel is beautiful in time, civilization is anytime, anywhere.*

旅游 is the Chinese word for *travel, trip, tourism*. 旅 has an ideographic of a man travelling with a pack on his back. 游 means *to swim, to walk, to roam*; its ideographic is that to swimming freely through the seas.

In English *to travel* comes from the French word *travailler* (*to work*), indicating originally that to travel is to toil, to face difficulties and to be actively involved in one's activities.

文明是最美的风景—*Wén míng shì zuì měi de fēng jǐng*
Can be translated as: *Civilization is the most beautiful scenery.*

风景 is the Chinese word for *landscape, scenary* and serves as a metaphor in the discourse instrument. 风 translates as *wind, news, style* and *custom*. The character is formed on the basis of a sub-character for *a small table, how many* and another character for *to govern* and/or *to nurture*. 景 means *bright, circumstance, scenery*, with an ideographic of the sun rising over a city (see Fig. 2.6).

Fig. 2.6 Civilization is the most beautiful scenery

In English *scenery* relates to the word *scene*, which is from Greek *skēnē* (a wooden stage for actors), something that gives shade.

旅途漫漫，文明相伴—*Lǚ tú màn, wén míng xiāng bàn*
Can be translated as: *Bring civilization with long journey, (word-for-word translation) Long journey, accompanied by civilization.*

旅途 is *a journey, a trip* (reminder: the ideographic of a person travelling with a pack on their back). 途 translates as *the way, route, road* and contains sub-characters for *to walk* and for *surplus, remainder*.

In English, the word journey is from old French *journée*, a day's length, day's work or travel. *Journey* took on the meaning of travelling by land or sea in the fourteenth century.

2 APPROACHING INTERCULTURALITY: CULTURE AND CIVILIZATION...

讲文明话办文明事做文明人 创文明城—*Jiǎng wén míng huà, bàn wén míng shì, zuò wén míng rén, chuàng wén míng chéng*
Can be translated as: *Speak civilized words, do civilized things, be civilized people, create a civilized city.*

MISCELLANEOUS

文化衫—*Wén huà shān*
Can be translated as: *DIY/cultural T-shirt.*

The idea of the cultural T-shirt emerged in the U.S.A. in the 1950s and has become popular worldwide ever since (see Fig. 2.7). A cultural T-shirt is a piece of garment with printed patterns or texts on the front and/or

Fig. 2.7 A person wearing a coat that reads OTHERS—Happiness to make you sweet enough trials make

back sides. It became popular in China in the 1980s and is omnipresent today, with messages in Chinese and English dominating. Seen randomly on Chinese streets, cultural T-shirts with the following messages: "We are all feminists", "Silence is better than lies", "Reading enriches the mind".

文化创意产业—*Wén huà chuàng yì chǎn yè*
Can be translated as *Cultural and Creative Industries (CCI)*.

创意 means *creative*. 创 is based on a character for *barn* and *cabin* and a character for *knife*. 意 is *idea, meaning, thought, to think*, with two characters for *sound, pronunciation* and *heart* combined (the latter conveying the meaning).

To create in English is from Latin *creare* for *to make grow*. It relates to the Roman goddess of agriculture Ceres (identified with Greek Demeter).

文化创意产业 or CCI is a large business niche with creativity as its core activity (see Fig. 2.8). For example, it involves the performing arts, animation, visual art, design and advertising. Aspects of interculturality (e.g. mix, inspiration from other places/people/languages) are often found in CCI.

文化名片—*Wén huà míng piàn*
Can be translated as: *Cultural name card*.

名片 is a (business) card. It is composed of 名 for example, *a name, a place* and *famous*, with an ideographic of a name called out to hail someone at night. 片 with a pictographic of half a tree trunk, can translate as *film, to slice, area of water*.

This discourse instrument is used to refer to specific elements, aspects and identity markers for a place, a city, a region. It symbolizes the overall cultural image attached to them (e.g. the Imperial Palace used to represent Beijing) and used for place-branding to attract potential visitors/tourists (Anttiroiko, 2014).

汉服文化—*Hàn fú wén huà*
Can be translated as: *Hanfu culture*.

汉服 is the traditional Han Chinese dress. 汉 refers to the Han Minzu/'ethnic' group, the Chinese (language) or the Han dynasty (206 BCE–220 AD). It is a simplified form of the character for the Han river, and thus contains a sub-character for water.

2 APPROACHING INTERCULTURALITY: CULTURE AND CIVILIZATION... 47

Fig. 2.8 An example of exhibits of 文化创意产业, with a focus on Chinese Minzu elements

In 汉服文化, the following elements are said to be included: sacrificial clothing, royal clothing, public clothing, uniforms and accessories, dating back to Confucian times. These traditions have been revived over the past decade in China and they appear to be popular amongst young Chinese (see Fig. 2.9). In Europe, in a similar vein, some people recreate and reenact Mediaeval life, habits and clothing as a hobby and/or way of life

Fig. 2.9 Lady wearing a Hanfu dress

(Hartley, 2003). This return to the past often has to do with identity, roots and an interest in one's 'grand' past (Maffesoli, 1997).

红色文化—*Hóng sè wén huà*
Can be translated as: *Red culture.*

The Red Culture was created by the Communist Party of China during the revolutionary years and symbolizes a revolutionary spirit, with historical and cultural connotations. Red symbolizes the blood of the nation. 紅色 is both *red* and *revolutionary* in Chinese and can be subdivided as:

- 紅 for *red, popular, revolutionary* and is based on sub-characters for *silk, thread* and *labour, work*.
- 色 has an ideographic for what a person desires. Its meaning is *colour* but also *look* and *appearance*.

Pause

This chapter about change and exchange through 'Chinese stories of interculturality' was dedicated to two concepts that have been at the centre of discussions on the notion (see Jackson, 2020). Our aim here was not to define them in Chinese or in English—they are semantically plural—but to explore their use in different discourse instruments. While reading the sections of the chapter we note the richness of the discourse instruments and realize that they can teach us about different aspects of interculturality *glocally*, that is, we can all identify with what they urge us to reflect on.

The word *culture* is accompanied by a long list of terms in the instruments: Accomplishment, awareness, belonging (sense of), commonsense, competence, cultivation, education, gene, inner quality, knowledge, literacy, self-awareness, self-cultivation, subjectivity, and translation. Each of the elements reveals specific functions of *culture* in Chinese in making us unthink and rethink interculturality in the English language.

Several discourse instruments were also presented as means of helping us analyse specific cultural phenomena: Construction, deposits, discount, heritage, innovation, loaded words, localization, output, people-to-people exchange, pollution, renaissance, revival, strong country, vocabulary. We have discussed the potential misunderstandings see controversies around some of these terms. Refraining from judging these instruments while reflecting on why we might feel uncomfortable with them—and the somewhat misleading power of the concepts of culture and civilization—appears to be an important aspect of working on change and exchange while engaging with 'Chinese stories' (see Han, 2019 on teaching culture in Chinese as a foreign language).

Figure 2.10 is a summary of our discussions in this chapter. It indicates how three themes are interrelated in the discourse instruments: the

Fig. 2.10 Chapter summary (culture and civilization)

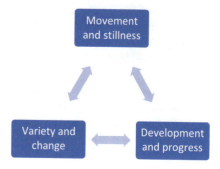

contradictory but powerful continuum of *movement and stillness, variety and change* as well as the ideas of *development and progress*, which are central in Chinese ideologies today—like in other contexts but they may be voiced under other notions such as *social justice, equality, well-being* and so on.

Our reflections on interculturality as change and exchange are fully supported by the discourse instruments of this chapter. Complementary discussions to come include: the content of change in interculturality, its advantages and drawbacks, the links between change and identity, people's justifications for change, the acceptance and refusal of change and well as preparation for analysing the influence on power relations on change (e.g. the power of 'money' and 'symbolic power').

> Thinking Further
>
> – Did you learn anything new about the concepts of culture and civilization while reading this chapter?
> – What types of 'cultural commonsense' (general knowledge) about your own culture should be known to reach a moderate level of acquaintance with your country? Can you give some examples?
> – How many groups can you clearly identify with (groups that are central to determine important aspects of your identity)? What 'cultural' elements provide you with a sense of belonging to these groups? Can you list and describe them?

(continued)

(continued)

- How could we balance respecting our own culture and opening up to other cultural elements? Can you think of successful examples?
- What do you think of the idea of 'cultural pollution'? Does it make sense to you? Can you think of other ways to express this idea? Is there an equivalent in other contexts that you are aware of, and which may not contain the word 'pollution'?
- Who uses the words civilization and/or civilized in your context? Why do they use them and what do they do with them? Do you sometimes hear yourself use them?
- For one day, write down all the messages, symbols and/or pictures that you see on people's cultural T-shirts around you, what kinds of messages do you note? What do they tell us about what people wish to tell others? What do they tell us about their identity but also about today's world, societies? Finally, how would you call 'cultural T-shirts' in your language(s)?
- Do you think that 文化常识 (cultural literacy) should be a component of intercultural competence?
- What does the idea of a *culturally strong country* bring to your mind? Can you think of a country that you would label as such and explain why?
- Can you think of examples of 'cultural discount' from your own country? Have there been attempts at promoting certain aspects of your culture that have failed in other parts of the world? On the other hand, can you think of elements that have 'sold' very well and explain why they are popular?
- The discourse instruments in the section Use of Civilized/Civilization are translated word-for-word. Can you think of ways of translating them that would make them clearer, more 'suitable' for your own context, making sure that they can be understood by others?
- Most countries have promoted some form of cultural revival/renaissance in the past 30 years, can you identify examples and explain what they were about and why?

(continued)

(continued)

- Many of the discourse instruments of this section hint at the fact that we need to navigate between stillness and movement in our lives. What do you make of this idea? Can you think of daily examples that illustrate this somewhat contradictory—but realistic—argument?
- Can you make a list of 文化词汇 (culture-loaded words) that you are aware of?
- Think of the word *development* (as in *economic development*): how often do you hear it and who uses it around you? What does it mean for them and who do they apply it to?
- A very difficult question: What does the idea of a 'backward culture' mean to you? Many of us feel uncomfortable with this discourse instrument, can you explain why and try to think of why some people find the instrument useful to think about the world—and potentially interculturality today?
- One Chinese student chose the following discourse instrument as one of the most important ones for interculturality: "'The ocean is vast because it admits all rivers' (海纳百川 有容乃大), which lies on the basis of cross-cultural realization. It means to respect and tolerate the diversity of civilizations and their respective cultural connotations and avoid judging the merits and disadvantages of cultures with rigid criteria and single perspective, such as ideology, political system and religious belief". What do you make of this instrument? Explain it and discuss how it relates to thinking about interculturality.

References

Anttiroiko, A.-V. (2014). *The Political Economy of City Branding*. Routledge.

Chemla, K., & Fox Keller, E. (2017). *Cultures Without Culturalism: The Making of Scientific Knowledge*. Duke University Press Books.

Dervin, F. (2016). *Interculturality in Education: A Theoretical and Methodological Toolbox*. Palgrave Macmillan.

Dervin, F., & Jacobsson, A. (2021). *Teacher Education for Critical and Reflexive Interculturality*. Palgrave Macmillan.

Dervin, F., & Risager, K. (2017). *Researching Identity and Interculturality.* Springer.
Eco, U. (2001). *Experiences in Translation.* University of Toronto Press.
Eriksen, T. H. (2001). Between Universalism and Relativism: 'A Critique of the UNESCO Concept of Culture'. In J. K. Cowan, M.-B. Dembour, & R. A. Wilson (Eds.), *Culture and Rights. Anthropological Perspectives* (pp. 127–148). Cambridge University Press.
Eriksen, T. H. (2016). *Overheating: An Anthropology of Accelerated Change.* Pluto.
Fang, W. (2019). *Modern Notions of Civilization and Culture in China.* Palgrave Macmillan.
Fei, X. (2015). *Globalization and Cultural Self-Awareness.* Springer.
Freire, J. (2021). *Nation Branding in Europe.* Routledge.
Gaukroger, S. (2020). *Civilization and the Culture of Science: Science and the Shaping of Modernity, 1795-1935.* Oxford University Press.
Han, J. (2019). *Theorising Culture: A Chinese Perspective.* Palgrave Macmillan.
Hartley, D. (2003). *Medieval Costume and How to Recreate It.* Dover Publications.
Huntington, S. P. (2002). *The Clash of Civilisations: And the Remaking of World order.* Simon & Schuster.
Jackson, J. (2020). *The Routledge Handbook of Language and Intercultural Communication.* Routledge.
Maffesoli, M. (1997). *The Time of the Tribes.* Sage.
Zheng, Z. (2019). 中国历史常识 *(General Knowledge of Chinese literature).* Tiandi Press.

CHAPTER 3

Exploring and Explaining Experiences of Interculturality

Introduction

When 'doing' interculturality, it is important to be able to place words behind what we experience, think, analyse and strategize. 'Doing' interculturality here means observing, analysing and self-reflecting on what happens when people from different 'places' or who simply appear to be different, get together. The ways we do all these can be uttered for oneself to self-reflect and act upon our 'inner dialogues' (as in "I should have behaved differently") and/or for others (e.g. "when you said that, it helped me rethink my initial ideas") to work together towards interculturality as co-construction and change.

The Chinese discursive instruments presented in this chapter concern both macro-contexts (e.g. at a larger economic-political level) and the concrete micro-context of interaction (e.g. in a classroom or a café). Putting words behind what is happening between us is a first step to enrich our ways of dealing with the complexity of the world, others and ourselves and to start examining, questioning, and… changing! Obviously, words are sometimes treacherous and the understanding and explanations that they offer might mislead us. Therefore, it is important to also keep a critical and reflexive eye towards the phrases and expressions proposed below.

© The Author(s), under exclusive license to Springer Nature Switzerland AG 2022
M. Yuan et al., *Change and Exchange in Global Education*, Palgrave Studies on Chinese Education in a Global Perspective,
https://doi.org/10.1007/978-3-031-12770-0_3

They are at times polysemic and unstable in meaning. What is more, they do not necessarily have a direct equivalent in other languages, which might influence the way we understand what they advocate.

Confronting our own beliefs, ideologies and experiences with the discursive instruments can also help us look at ourselves in the mirror and investigate things differently. Before judging the content of the instruments, ponder over them critically. Usually what opposes our own beliefs and sense of experience can help us go deeper into our reflections—and thus enrich future experiences!

As always, keep a reflective and critical eye open!

The following instruments are introduced:

(a) Tools to analyse interculturality from a macro-perspective to understand and explain certain aspects of interculturality such as dialogue, domination, mistreatment and competition. These revolve mostly around the concept of culture introduced in the previous chapter.

(b) Tools to understand and explain interculturality, and how we experience it, from a personal and/or micro-perspective. This concerns our own individual and complex engagement with the multifacetedness of interculturality.

Tools to Analyse Interculturality from a Macro-perspective and Its Potential Consequences on Interpersonal Communication

Reflecting on broader perspectives of interculturality is a good starting point for preparing for more interpersonal and contextualized situations of encounter. Like any situation of sociality, interculturality is dominated by fluidity and even inconsistency in the ways people negotiate discourses, identities, representations of themselves, others, places, things, and so on (Bauman, 2014). However, unequal power relations tend to solidify interculturality and lead conversations and negotiations in one-way directions, dominated by powerful voices. These tools can help us unthink and rethink such elements at macro- and micro-levels. Through our awareness, we might be able to think deeper and take hypothetical actions against them, if need be.

文化自大—*Wén huà zì dà.*
Can be translated as: *Cultural arrogance.*

The word *arrogance* usually triggers bad sentiments in the one who experiences it. For the American dictionary the *Merriam Webster*, *arrogance* represents "an insulting way of thinking or behaving that comes from believing that you are better, smarter, or more important than other people". Arrogance is insulting, abusing, upsetting in the sense that it creates an (unfair) hierarchy between people, ideas, things, as decided upon by one of the parties only. One can easily imagine how this could disrupt interculturality.

What *arrogance* means in what we utter in intercultural encounters is not easy to define though, since some people might find certain statements on 'us' and 'them' to be 'true', 'modest', while others might see them as 'arrogant', 'inventions'—even 'insulting'. To indicate what it might feel (for us) we could say that one is in/directly 'put down', made to feel inferior and embarrassed, by a positivizing statement about someone's cultural affiliation and characteristics. By hearing the statement, one is made to think about one's culture in a negative and disapproving way. We note that the utterer's intentions might not have been to trigger this kind of feeling.

In English *arrogance* comes from Latin *arrogantia* for *presumption, pride, haughtiness*.

In Chinese 自大 (arrogance) is composed of 自, which means *self, oneself*, but also *from, since, naturally, surely* and 大 which represents a man with outstretched arms. 自 has a pictographic of a nose (to refer to oneself one (used to) point(s) to one's nose in China).

文化自大 can be used to refer to both macro- or micro-levels of interaction. When someone or an entity projects an image of being better, superior, for example, more civilized and advanced than another, looking down upon them. This can be done in direct (e.g. "in my culture, we are politer than others") or subtle ways (e.g. "the happiest country in the world"). Cultural arrogance might have to do with marketing (country branding whereby a country is marketed like a product) and the ethnocentric education one might have received since childhood from school, parents and 'local' media. In general, cultural arrogance is damaging for one of the parties in contact, since they are described indirectly as somewhat inferior—to diverse degrees. Sometimes, one might use other people's cultural arrogance to put our own 'culture' down (e.g. "American culture is politer than our Finnish culture").

Although 文化自大 is omnipresent and found behind for example, *ethnocentrism* (believing that one's country is at the centre of the world) and *banal nationalism* (making statements about one's superiority in a way that seems to make them natural, Billig, 1995), it must be deconstructed, analysed and exposed whenever possible. Acting upon it is also a necessity at macro- and micro-levels of interculturality, should the opportunity emerge. Responding to cultural arrogance by one's own (cultural) arrogance—for example, listing one's own superior characteristics—is usually a first step but it may not be the best option. Helping the other to see themselves in the mirror and observe 'quality' in others might be more rewarding in the long run. At the same time, it is also important for each of us to reflect on how our own discourses of culture might pass as cultural arrogance to others and give the impression that we are superior (e.g. "people are very honest in my culture"; "my people are super clever"). We need to remember that no one is immune against cultural arrogance and that statements about 'us' and 'them' often contain traces of such arrogance. Finally, *cultural arrogance* can also apply to 'locality' and be exhibited by people from our own country who (have been made to) believe they are better than others, for example, in the way they speak a 'national' language in a standard way versus a dialect.

外国的月亮比中国的圆—*Wài guó de yuè liàng bǐ zhōng guó de yuán*

This discursive instrument translates as, "the foreign moon is rounder than the Chinese moon". It indicates a belief of superiority of the other, while presenting an inferior image of one's own culture and group. This belief often relates to someone who has spent time in another country. It goes hand in hand with the idea of *arrogance* found in the previous instrument, but emerges from the one who does not belong or cannot claim affiliation with the country being constructed as better. Although it is impossible to find the origin of this instrument, it is often found in critiques of Chinese people being attracted to 'everything foreign'—and negating the achievements and 'beauty' of Chinese culture—but also in discourses about the need to learn from the outside world (especially the West, and more specifically, the U.S.). Being inspired and influenced by other parts of the world is not something to be systematically combated, feared and/or ignored but it must be unthought, discussed and weighed with people we identify with and others. If the 'foreign moon' leads to discrimination, injustice, a sense of loss and disrupted identity, it should then be resisted.

Finally, we argue that when people believe that the 'moon is rounder' elsewhere, the reasons why they believe so tell us more about them (who they are, their worldviews, their self-perceptions and maybe their illusions) than about what is 'better' in another country. Statements about better and worse are often tainted with hypersubjectivity.

The character 国 (guó) means *country, nation, state*. Its ideographic is that of a treasure 玉 within a country's borders 囗. 中国 (zhōngguó) is China, with 中 referring to the *centre, middle, within* (a line 丨 through the centre of a box 口). 外国 (Wàiguó) is a *foreign country*, with 外 referring to *the outside, foreign, external*. Its ideographic is night-time 夕 divinations 卜 (i.e. the supernatural, the foreign).

月 (yuè) is the *moon* but also *month*, with a pictographic of a crescent moon.

文化渗透—*Wén huà shèn tòu.*
Can be translated as: *Cultural infiltration, penetration, but also, cross-fertilization of culture.*

This discursive instrument is a great illustration of interculturality as change, movement and re-creation. It is also very much indicative of power relations: when one 'cultural' element infiltrates another way of doing, thinking, behaving, not all elements win, even in the cross-fertilization indicated by the phrase. One always dominates, even if minimally. 文化渗透 is also used to refer to a 'strong culture' influencing, penetrating into a 'less powerful one'. It emphasizes the importance of observing power relations in relation to interculturality and to problematize the creation of new cultural aspects when two entities meet. Sometimes the term is used to refer simply to cultures feeding into each other. In research terms, referring to power imposition of one culture onto another such as *Starbucksification* (Wong, 2015) or *MacDonaldization* (Ritzer, 1993) can serve as synonyms. Without any indication of problematic power relations, the ideas of *hybridity, mixing* and/or *mélange* could also be used as synonyms.

渗透 means *to permeate, to seep into, to penetrate.* 渗 shèn *to seep, to ooze, to horrify*, is composed of 氵 (shuǐ) for *water* and 参 (cān) for *to take part in, to intervene, and ginseng.* 透 tòu means *to penetrate, to pass through, thoroughly, completely, transparent, to appear, to show.* This character is composed of 辶 (chuò) for *to walk; walking* and 秀 (xiù) for *elegant, graceful, refined, flowing, luxurian.* In Chinese, these characters have a direct link to *water* and *flowing.*

In the English language, *to penetrate* comes from Latin *penetratus, to out or get into, enter into, cause to go into* and *penus, the innermost part of a temple, store of food, food provisions*. The more figurative sense in English is from the sixteenth century: *to influence, to gain intellectual access*. *To infiltrate* might come from the French *infiltrer* which refers to penetrate enemy lines, and also refers to fluids. In the English language, there is a reference to foods and water.

We note, referring back to Chap. 2, that cross-fertilization is, in a sense, innate to culture, since culture changes, adapts, and is moulded constantly by relating it to other cultures. This can happen peacefully, but also through harsh negotiations, violence, and so on.

What to do about 文化渗透 is a question for decision-makers and, marginally but importantly, individuals. One can decide to accept, reject or ignore certain cultural practices that are 'penetrating' our daily lives—but often in vain since cultural elements are so fluid. Some countries have clear rules about limiting penetration. For example, in France radio channels must play at least 35% of songs in French to stem the encroachment of English.

文化入侵—*Wénhuà rùqīn*

Can be translated as: *Cultural invasion/aggression*.

As asserted in the second chapter, the main characteristic of 'culture' is that it changes, transforms and is moulded in contact with other cultures. We have also seen in earlier discursive instruments in this chapter that these actions do not always take place in a vacuum and/or in a happily and jointly agreed way. Cultural invasion/aggression consists in conquering another 'place' through imposed one-way transformations. Obvious but also invisible change is imposed through this type of invasion, which can be soft and/or violent. Imperialism as described by Edward Said (1979) is an ideal-type of 文化入侵.

All kinds of pressures can occur, ideological, political, economic, technological, attitudinal, behavioural ones (amongst others), and have an influence on our lives, ways of thinking, relations. Our global history has witnessed constant cultural invasion/aggression through all kinds of conflicts and wars. Examples of such invasions include (randomly): the use of PPT in education which can format the way we think and present thinking to others in simplistic ways; the widespread use of global rankings in different aspects of our lives (from happiness to the value of passports); the imposition of calendars and celebrations (Christmas, Halloween). Different countries and different parts of the world have responded differently to 文化入侵, with some in ways that demonstrate a more liberal and self-confident way.

Feelings of unfair 文化入侵 can trigger acts of chauvinism and nationalism as counter-reactions, which might lead to rejection of the other, boycott of a given country and illusionary feelings of superiority.

Later in the book, we will discuss the 'companion term' *cultural self-confidence* (入侵, wénhuà zìxìn), which offers one way of unthinking 文化入侵.

入侵 in Chinese means *to invade, to intrude* and is composed of the characters 入 (rù) for *to enter, to go into, to join, to become a member of,* with an ideographic of an arrow indicating 'enter', and 侵 (qīn) for *to invade, to encroach, to infringe, to approach.*

文化竞争力—*Wén huà jìng zhēng lì*
Can be translated as: *Cultural competitiveness.*

The idea of *competing* might sound 'non-intercultural', see 'anti-intercultural'. However, in an era of liberalism and market-dominated mentality, cultures have become products and ideas that have a value on the 'market'. When one answers the question 'where are you from?', one gives away an idea about our value on the world stage. The name of a country will provide our interlocutors with certain (wrong) ideas and ideologies about our 'culture'. Depending on where we are located in the world, and on the 'country branding' that we have been exposed to, value will be attributed to the ones we meet: *civilized, modern, hard-working, beautiful, clever,* etc. Often, we transfer these misrepresentations to the individuals whom we meet—as much as they might transfer the ones they have (been forced to) invent about us.

In the discursive instrument under review, 竞争力 (jìng zhēng lì) translates as *competitiveness.* 竞 (jìng) means *to compete, to contend, to struggle* and has an ideographic for *to stand up* 立 *to a foe* 兄. 争, zhēng, can be translated in English as *to strive for, to vie for, to argue or debate,* but also *deficient or lacking.* The ideographic of 争 is *two hands* 爪 and ⺕ *fighting over* 丨. Finally, 力 (lì) has the following equivalents in English: *power, force, strength, ability,* and the adverb *strenuously.* Its ideographic is a *plough's head* representing strength.

To summarize, 文化竞争力 refers to the ability to compete with other cultures, to offer new, fresh and better ideas, artefacts than others or at least at the same level as cultures fantasized to be 'top' ones. It also hints at the ability to influence other cultures and to be legitimate for it. As asserted earlier, economic aspects are included in this term too. The consequences of treating cultures as competitive, especially financially speaking, can be many and varied and must be carefully analysed and—if possible—countered.

Finally, we note that 文化竞争力 is also used in the corporate world, that is, shared concepts, beliefs, values and rules of a given company that promote belonging and togetherness. Through adopting and nurturing these elements, a company can be more competitive on the market (Mukherjee & He, 2014).

文化强国—*Wénhuà qiángguó*
Can be translated as: *Cultural power*.

强国 refers to a powerful country. The word-for-word translation is thus *powerful cultural country*.

In China, this discursive instrument emerged during the Fifth Plenary Session of the 19th Central Committee of the Communist Party of China in October 2020, with the emphasis on putting forward the long-term goal of building a cultural power by 2035. What *culture* means here refers to the continued integration of Marxism in socialism with Chinese characteristics in, for example, Mao Zedong Thought, the theoretical system of socialism with Chinese characteristics, and Xi Jinping Thought on Socialism with Chinese Characteristics for a New Era.

In daily life, the discursive instrument might be used to describe cultural self-confidence and attraction to the outside world.

文化软实力—*Wén huà ruǎn shí lì*
Can be translated as: *Cultural soft power*.

(From one of our students) "this means that culture is part of the soft power of a country. We should transform excellent cultural traditional resources into powerful realistic productive forces. Cultural productions, ideas and artefacts become allies to promoting e.g. a country economic-politically".

软实力 is *soft power*: 软 (ruǎn) *soft; flexible*, used for example, in 软件 (ruǎn jiàn) for *computer software*, composed of 车 (chē) *for a cart, vehicle, to move in a cart* and 欠 (qiàn) for *to lack, to owe, to breathe, to yawn*. 实力 (shí lì) is composed of 实 for *real, true, honest, really, solid; fruit, seed*, and *definitely* and 力 (lì) for *power, force, strength, ability, strenuously*. Ideographic: A plough's head representing strength.

Cultural soft power is part of many countries' strategies to present themselves to the world and have some global influence. For China, cultural soft power relates to the realization of the Chinese dream of the great rejuvenation of the Chinese Nation, as proposed by General Secretary Xi Jinping: striving to spread contemporary Chinese values, to showcase the uniqueness of Chinese culture, and to improve the international 'power to speak'. Joseph Nye (1990) was the first one to propose the concept in English. All powerful Western countries have used their cultural soft power over the past two centuries to influence the world by setting up for example, cultural and language centres in other countries. The *Alliance Française* and *British Council* are examples of cultural soft power initiatives from France and Britain.

Understanding and Explaining Interculturality from a Personal and/or Micro-perspective

In this subsection we focus on discursive instruments that can help us as individuals to reflect on our own experiences and encounters within interculturality. These include reflecting on our transformations, disorientation, perspective-taking, and attitudes towards others.

十年树木, 百年树人—*Shí nián shù mù, bǎinián shù rén*
Can be translated as: *It takes ten years to grow trees, but a hundred to rear people.*

We include this first discursive instrument as an important reminder to us all: interculturality is a never-ending story; no one can ever claim to be fully ready for it and even to teach about it—which would mean that some of us are somewhat 'invincible'; and when one feels that one might be ready for it, we are 'unready'. We should persevere, question our assumptions and assumptions of our assumptions and never be satisfied with the way we conceptualize, problematize and 'do' interculturality. Self-reflection, experiencing, discussing, disagreeing, asking for clarification and help, are part of this lifelong learning process.

This discursive instrument is from one of the earliest Chinese philosophers called Guan Zhong (c. 716–645 BCE). It reminds us that we should endeavour to lifelong training and learning and never consider that we can claim to be ever ready.

For interculturality, one could never say, "I am ready to meet any person on this planet and 'deal with' them properly, effectively."

木 is a tree in Chinese.

多元化—*Duōyuán huà*

Can be translated as: *pluralism, diversification, multiculturalism.*

The ideas of *diversity, pluralism* and *multiculturalism* are central to reflecting on interculturality. However, these terms can mean different things to different people, for example, in terms of who is included in them (*insiders/outsiders, minority/majority*) and what characteristic is taken into account (Culture? Diversity? Language? Race?).

In Chinese the term contains 多 (composed of 夕 meaning *night*), which refers to *many/much, numerous, more, multi-*; 元 to *perspectives, parts* (but also to *the Chinese currency unit*) and 化 *to transform, change into*—which is contained in the idea of *culture* in Chinese, 文化 (wénhuà).

The term 多元化 could be used to refer to 'diversification of diversity' and superdiversity in English, since it includes several tautological hints at *different parts* and *change*.

异境茫然—*Yì jìng máng rán.*

Can be translated as: *Change of scenery, depaysement, disorientation.*

When one goes abroad and gets into 'obvious' interculturality (interculturality is always all around us but it can appear more apparent when we cross borders), one can experience this as mere (pleasant, exhilarating) change of scenery but also as a difficult episode of depaysement or even disorientation. Putting these feelings into words is an important aspect of any intercultural experience: what do we miss abroad? What in the new environment do we feel is pleasant, hard to get used to, beautiful/ugly? At the same time, what similarities might make us forget the difficulty of getting used to this new place?

异境 refers to *a foreign land.* 异 (yì) can mean *different, other, hetero-, unusual, strange, surprising,* but also *to distinguish, to separate, to discriminate*. The ideographic of 异 is a simplified form of 異: a person 共 with a scary face 田. 境 (jìng) translates as *border, place, condition, boundary, circumstances, territory*. The character is subdivided in characters that make direct references to soil and earth. 边境 (biān jìng) is *the frontier, the border* and 境外 (jìng wài) a reference to *outside (a country's) borders*. The term 茫然 is translated as *blankly, vacantly, at a loss*, with 茫 (máng), *vast, with no clear boundary*, and figuratively *hazy, indistinct, unclear, confused*. 艹 (cǎo) is *grass, weed, plant, herb*. 然 (rán) corresponds to *correct, right, so, thus, like this, -ly* and hints at *dog meat* and *fire*, through its subcomponents.

The feeling of not being at home, which can be both a positive and/or negative feeling that changes as one experiences another place, can apply to being located abroad or in one's own country—in a new place in any case. The English word, from the French, indicates being outside one's country (*pays* = country in French) and potentially being within a different landscape (*paysage* = landscape). In Chinese, the reference is to a 'foreign land', which is different, unusual, strange.

四海为家—*Sìhǎi wéi jiā*
Can be translated as: *to regard the four corners of the world all as home.*

The idiom 四海为家 translates word-for-word with 'four seas are home'. To consider the four seas as home is to be a cosmopolitan, someone who can live anywhere and feel at home. Four seas refer to the whole world here (四海).

As a footnote, let us remind ourselves that being a 'cosmopolitan' is an ideal rather than a reality. The illusion of being able to adapt 'everywhere', to be open to and to tolerate anything, must be discussed in education. The ideologies of the 'citizen of the world' and 'the global citizen' are problematic by the hierarchy they create (subconsciously). When such phrases are used, it is always interesting to note who utters them and for whom—and what they tell us about the ideological use of such terms.

入境问俗—*Rù jìng wèn sú*
Can be translated as: *Enter the realm of other countries, first ask about their ban; when entering the capitals of other countries, ask their customs first.* This discursive instrument might also be translated simply in English by the word *immigration*.

入 translates as *enter;* 境, territory; 问 is *to ask* and 俗 refers to the words *vulgar, custom.*

This was a piece of advice found in *The Book of Rites* (礼记), a series of texts describing administration, social rules and ceremonial rites of the Zhou Dynasty (eleventh to third centuries B.C.E.). In order to minimize breaking taboos, embarrassing oneself or others through ignorance, it is better to ask questions about practices, views, discursive worlds, relations, when one meets others rather than make assumptions about what one sees, hears and/or experiences. Learning by exploring and making mistakes can be a good thing in interculturality, but when one can do so by entering into dialogues with the other, one might benefit more. By showing curiosity, this might favour cooperation and trust-building.

潜移默化—*Qiányímòhuà*

Can be translated as: *imperceptibly, silent transformations, unknowingly changing.*

Originally derived from *The Family Instructions of Master Yan*, a book by the Confucian scholar Yan Zhitui (531–591 AD), this discursive instrument reminds us that we go through quiet and unconscious transformations when we experience new things (e.g. other people, a specific environment), get used to them and 'absorb' them in us. Unknowingly we change. Living abroad, being surrounded by people who might behave, think and speak differently, without noticing, we might—and they might—adopt different ways, or mix ours and their ways resulting in a hybrid form. Reviewing a personal diary kept over a long period of time can reveal such 'silent transformations' and help us become aware of our own tolerance for change.

潜移默化 is composed of the following Chinese characters:

- 潜 (qián) can mean *latent, hidden, secret* and combines the subcharacters for *water* and *to change, to replace* and *to substitute for;*
- 移 (yí) refers to *shift, move, alter, change* and includes characters for *cereal, grain, rice, plant* and for *much, many, multi-, more than* (as in the word for diversity in Chinese);
- 默 (mò) is the character for *silent, tacit, to write from memory.* Its pictographic consists of a dog 犬 watching in the dark 黑. 默契 (mò qì) is a discursive instrument used to indicate *tacit understanding,*

mutual understanding, rapport, connected at a deep level with each other, (of team members) well coordinated;
- Finally, 化 (huà) translates as *change into, transform, melt* (also as *-ization* in English). As a reminder this somewhat omnipresent character, shares the same ending as the word for *culture* in Chinese: 文化 (wénhuà).

In this discursive instrument, we identify many (repetitive) indications of changing, moving, transforming and multiplicity—which fits well with the very idea of interculturality.

不识庐山真真面目，只缘身在此山中—*Lú shān zhēn miàn mù*
Can be translated as: *I see not the true face of Mount Lushan as I am right in it.*

This is from a poem by Su Shi (1037–1101) about his visit to Mount Lu (Lushan) in Jiangxi Province (southeastern China). He is looking at the Mount, and reflecting on what he sees, he argues that he cannot claim to see the true features of the mountain so close and that, if he was standing at a different distance, he would see it differently.

The 'true face' of the Mount is a metaphor for failing to see the truth about a person or a matter, especially if one is involved, one cannot see the situation clearly. Another interpretation is that one needs to look at a reality from different perspectives.

Interculturality is always about perceptions—to be more precise—misperceptions. There are many ways of seeing and interpreting realities, behaviours, attitudes, discourses, etc. One should always look at the 'Mount' of interculturality from different angles, and not assume that closeness to the Mount or 'acquired knowledge' are enough to get a full grip over what one hears, sees, smells, witnesses. We thus need to be open to testing our senses, impressions, pre-conceived explanations and perceptions.

张飞穿针 - 粗中有细—*Zhāng fēi cìzhēn cūxì*
Can be translated as: *Zhang Fei piercing needle—thick but thin.*

Zhang Fei was a general in the State of Shu (Southwest China; 167–221 AD) who was usually represented as rough and harsh. What the discursive instrument suggests is that Zhang Fei could also be seen as refine, cautious and careful in his own roughness and rudeness.

粗中有细 means *refine in one's rough ways.*

When we 'do' interculturality, we often tend to observe others through our own lenses, and we often end up judging them based on our own 'ways'. This person is seen as 'rude', that one more 'civilized', etc. There are no objective criteria for these elements; they always rely on our own pre-determined sense of politeness, development, etc. Take politeness as an example: there is no universally agreed upon definition and description of what is rude and not.

Like the previous discursive instrument, there is thus a need to observe, comment upon and thus judge others from different angles. *Rough* and *refine* may mean different things to different people. What is more they may not be clearly separated.

井里的蛤蟆-没见过大天—*Jǐng lǐ de hámá-méi jiàn guo dà tiān*

Can be translated as: *A frog in a well—never having seen the whole sky.*

This discursive instrument also reminds us that we need to step outside our comfort zone and to look out to the other. Here the metaphor is about a frog being unable to see what is happening outside the well it is stuck in—having access to a small portion of the sky. Without being able to jump out of, its vision of the world is limited.

This discursive instrument is often used to mock people with narrow horizons and limited knowledge. For interculturality, this tells us to open up our sights towards the larger sky, to see the world from different and broader perspectives (again!), and if possible, to jump out of our well. When and if this happens, we might understand the other better, sympathize with them and start looking at oneself in the mirror.

大天 is the Chinese for the 'big sky'.

尊重—*Zūn zhòng*

Can translate as: *Respect, value, to esteem, to respect, to honour, to value, eminent, serious, proper.*

The idea of respect as an expected outcome of and objective for interculturality is often put forward in the literature (Fisher-Yoshida & Geller, 2009; for Chinese see e.g. Han, 2019). Unfortunately, respect is not a straightforward notion in English and other languages. It is thus important to reflect on its multilingual meanings and connotations.

In English, the word *respect* comes from Latin *respectus* for *regard, a looking at*. The phrase *with all due respect*, which introduces polite disagreement, is from the seventeenth century.

In Chinese, 尊 (zūn) means *senior, of a senior generation, to honour, to respect* but also 尊 is *a classifier for cannons and statues, ancient wine vessel*. A hand 寸 making an offering of wine 酋 is its ideographic. 重 (zhòng) has as an ideographic of a burden carried for a thousand 千 miles 里.

尊重 refers to a polite meeting and a sense of admiration between individuals, who are marked by hierarchical differences such as an employer and an employee. One of the two parties is considered as higher and deserving being valued. This type of respect corresponds to a way of saving face and does not necessarily involve reciprocity. This form of respect also refers to the respect of the younger generation to the elders or worship of a subordinate towards their superior.

尊敬—*Zūn jìng*
Can be translated as: *To respect; to revere*.

This other version of the idea of *respect* in Chinese helps us complexify the notion.

Its first character is the same as in the previous discursive instrument 尊重—zūn zhòng: 尊 (zūn) means *senior, of a senior generation, to honour, to respect* but also 尊 is a classifier for *cannons and statues, ancient wine vessel*. A hand 寸 making an offering of wine 酋 is its ideographic. 敬 jìng is defined as *to respect, to venerate, to salute, to offer*. The character is composed of characters hinting at carelessness, frivolity and illicitness and to rap, to tap and to let go.

This represents respect as a deep phenomenon, a feeling that builds up as one gets to meet, work and cooperate with another person. This feeling does not necessarily have to be reciprocal. This is respect as a process.

With these two versions of respect in Chinese, we see that there is a need to reflect openly on the 'flavours' of words when interacting multilingually so we can ensure minimum understanding between us (Eco, 2001). Respect can mean different things to different multilingual speakers.

会心—Huì xīn
Can be translated as: *Understanding each other without words; heart-to-heart communication.*

Reflecting on our relations with people from different countries can help us see that interculturality is not systematically so different from other forms of encounters, or more difficult. One interesting form of communication is described as *heart-to-heart* in Chinese.

会 (huì) stands for *knowing (of e.g. a smile, look)*. Its ideographic is people 人 speaking 云. 心 (xīn) refers to heart, mind, intention, centre, core in English. Its pictographic is that of a heart.

When people know each other very well, they do not necessarily need words to express their feelings or their opinions in order to understand each other. A blink of an eye, a smile, read properly by the other, can lead to spontaneous understanding. The reference to the heart in Chinese is derived from a feeling of harmony when 会心 takes place. This phrase is found in Liu Yiqing (403–444 A.D.). In his *New Account of Tales of the World*, the author collected anecdotes, short conversations and observations about important figures in China between 150 and 420 A.D. One could place 会心 at the centre of interculturality, when one has gained enough trust and knowledge of each other, heart-to-heart communication can begin.

人同此心，心同此理—Rén tóng cǐ xīn, xīn tóng cǐ lǐ
Can be translated as: *empathy, people have the same heart, the heart has the same reason.*

This discursive instrument is a quote from a scholar of the Southern Song Dynasty, Lu Jiuyuan (1139–1193). He argued that any human being shares the same values, truths and morals as others. This has been used to describe the exchanges between China and the 'West', with a view to understand both their similarities and differences. *Although there are differences, there will always be similarities*, is the main argument of this instrument.

We will come back to *differilitudes* (Dervin & Jacobsson, 2022), the enmeshment of similitude and difference in intercultural encounters, in the next chapter.

心 is the Chinese character for heart.

尺有所短, 寸有所长—*Chǐ yóu suǒ duǎn, cùn yóu suǒ cháng*
Can be translated as: *A foot may prove short while an inch may prove long; everyone has their weak and strong points.*

The instrument first appeared in the poetry of Qu Yuan (屈原, c. 339–278 B.C.E.) and is based on a metaphor used to show that every person or object has strong and weak points. In other words, nobody is perfect.

Another good reminder: when faced with intercultural situations, if unsuccessful, we may be tempted to judge others as 'inferior', 'uncivilized', 'impolite', etc. Opening up to viewing self and other differently, *we all have 'good' and 'weak' points*, represents an important and recurrent element in the discursive instruments discussed until now.

尽信书, 不如无书—*Jìn xìn shū, bùrú wú shū*
Can translate as: *It is better to believe in books than to have no books; be critical of what you read.*

This discursive instrument for interculturality is based on Mencius (孟子, 372–289 BCE), a follower of Confucius. The philosopher had read about a war, which he thought was just, and could not believe an account that presented it as a 'terrible event'. So, he asked his followers to not believe all that they read, and to analyse the words instead.

It is meant to encourage people to think critically, reflexively and independently instead of thinking mechanically and believing everything one reads, and taking printed words as dogma.

书 is the character for *book*, but also for *letter, script* and *calligraphy*.

Pause

In this chapter, we have examined two kinds of instruments: (1) Instruments that can support us in understanding and explaining central aspects of interculturality such as dialogue, mistreatment and competition; and (2) Instruments helping us reflect on how we experience interculturality as a real complex phenomenon.

For the first kind of instruments several 'negative' phenomena were deconstructed and discussed: the idea of 'The foreign moon is rounder than the Chinese moon' as well as (cultural) aggression, arrogance,

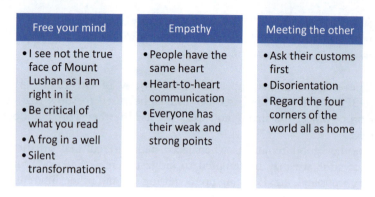

Fig. 3.1 Chapter summary (free your mind, empathy and meeting the other)

competitiveness, cross-fertilization of culture, infiltration, invasion, penetration, power, and soft power. The awareness of and continued reflexive and critical engagement with such issues can help us build up discursive 'power' to counter them in macro- (e.g. social media) and micro-contexts (e.g. when interacting with one individual) of interculturality.

Figure 3.1 summarizes the kinds of strategies offered from some of the discourse instruments. They are categorized into *free your mind*, *empathy* and *meeting the other*.

In present and future intercultural encounters, the reader might want to bear in mind both the kinds of challenges that 'doing' interculturality can trigger as well as the list of discourse instruments that can support us in attempting to move beyond them.

Thinking Further

- After reading this chapter, do you see a clearer link between 'culture', 'politics' and 'finance' in the way we 'do' interculturality and we have been made to think about interculturality?
- Can you think of examples of obvious and invisible 'cultural invasion' today and in the past?

(continued)

(continued)

- Can you remember a good example of 'cultural arrogance' that you have faced in interaction with someone from another country or another part of your own country?
- Interpersonally, if someone appears arrogant in terms of interculturality, what strategies could be adopted to 'counter-attack'?
- How does your country usually respond to 'cultural invasion/aggression'? Can you think of concrete examples from today and/or the past?
- Do you see the spread of Starbucks and other such companies as a threat? Explain.
- Do you feel that the 'moon' is generally speaking better, worse (or both) in other countries? Why (not)? Why would people think it is?
- Is there someone around you that you consider to be 'ready' to face interculturality without encountering too many problems? Why? And reflect on what makes them readier than you are.
- Everybody has experienced disorientation in a new place, one way or another. Can you recall one such instance and answer the following questions? How did you feel? Thinking back, what did you learn from feeling disoriented? What could you have done differently to make the experience less stressful? Do you feel readier for this kind of experience today? Why?
- Reflect on one important silent transformation that you have experienced in your life. How did it happen? When and how did you realize that you had changed?
- Have you ever experienced something that you felt was very 'rude' with a person from another country? Recall the event: how did it happen? How did you deal with it? When you think back about it, was it really 'rude' or something else? Have you yourself been rude to someone without realizing? How did you find out about it? What did you do to 'repair' the impression of rudeness you might have given?

(continued)

(continued)

- If you were an educator (maybe you are), how could you help your students look out of their 'wells' to view the entire sky, like the frog stuck in a well? How do we open up to other worlds?
- How many people can you understand 'without words'? Who are they? How long have you known them? How was the process of getting to know them so well? Are there people from other countries with whom you can have 'heart-to-heart' communication?
- How do you define the very idea of *respect*? Can you think of examples of when you use the term to deal with other people? Why do you use it and how? How does it relate to the two different Chinese terms presented in the chapter?
- In the introduction we mentioned one discourse instrument (邯郸学步) presented by one of our students, which, in English, translates as *Handan Toddler, learning to walk in Handan, learning a style of walking*, or: *imitating others and thus losing one's own individuality*. Think about critiques of globalization that you have heard in the media (e.g. about Starbucks, Macdonald's): how do these relate to 邯郸学步?

References

Bauman, Z. (2014). *Identity*. Polity.
Billig, M. (1995). *Banal Nationalism*. Sage.
Dervin, F., & Jacobsson, A. (2022). *Intercultural Communication Education. Broken Realities and Rebellious Dreams*. Springer.
Eco, U. (2001). *Experiences in Translation*. University of Toronto Press.
Fisher-Yoshida, B., & Geller, K. D. (2009). *Transnational Leadership Development: Preparing the Next Generation for the Borderless Business World*. AMACOM.
Han, J. (2019). *Theorising Culture: A Chinese Perspective*. Palgrave Macmillan.
Mukherjee, A., & He, H. (2014). Company Identity and Marketing: An Integrative Framework. *Journal of Marketing Theory and Practice, 16*(2), 111–125.

Nye, J. (1990). Soft Power. *Foreign Policy, 80,* 153–171.
Ritzer, G. (1993). *The MacDonaldization of Society.* Sage.
Said, E. (1979). *Orientalism.* Pantheon Books.
Wong, N. C. W. (2015). Starbuckization. In D. T. Cook & M. Ryan (Eds.), *The Wiley Blackwell Encyclopedia of Consumption and Consumer Studies* (pp. 1–2). Wiley Blackwell.

CHAPTER 4

'Doing' Interculturality Together

INTRODUCTION

In this chapter, the discourse instruments suggest specific ways of thinking about and doing interculturality together. The focus is on the micro-level of direct and/or mediated interaction (e.g. via social media). Three essential principles of interculturality, which have been highlighted in international research umpteen times (e.g. Abdallah-Pretceille, 2006; Piller, 2010; Dervin, 2016, 2017; Ferri, 2018) are described: *harmony from a constructivist perspective; the continuum of difference-similarity; reciprocity.*

We start with general elements that can help us reflect on how to position oneself ethically speaking, towards intercultural encounters: non-violence, harmonious coexistence and tolerance.

非攻—*Fēi gōng*
Can be translated as: *Opposing and denouncing unjust warfare, non-attack.*

非 (fēi) means *to not be, not, wrong, incorrect, non-, un-, in-* but also *to reproach* or *blame*. The character is sometimes used as an abbreviation for 非洲, *Africa*. Its ideographic represents the wings of two opposed birds, two people back-to-back. 攻 (gōng) is *to attack, to accuse, to study*. The character is composed of other characters expressing *labour, work* and *to rap* and *tap*.

This Mohist concept urges people to adopt a non-aggressive attitude. It constituted Mozi's view of war in the early days of the Warring States Period (475–221 B.C.E.), a period of division in Ancient China. 非攻 also denounces immoral wars between nations. It refers directly to the need to avoid attacks and thus to adopt 'universal love' to build a harmonious society. Non-violence is rarely discussed in direct relation to interculturality but it has been problematized in diversity psychology and education (e.g. Kool & Agrawal, 2020).

协和万邦—*Xié hé wàn bāng*
Can be translated as: *Harmonious coexistence of all.*
Can be used as an idiom meaning *'To make all nations live together peacefully'.*

协 (xié) means *to cooperate, to harmonize, to help, to assist, to join* and is composed of sub-characters referring to *ten, tenth, complete, perfect* as well as *to set up, to manage, to run, to handle.* The second character 和 (hé) contains hints at *cereal, grain, rice, plant* and 口 (kǒu) for *mouth, entrance, gate, and opening.* 万 (wàn) is the character for *one, a, an; alone.* And the final character 邦 (bāng) means *country, nation, state* and has an ideographic for a bountiful place.

From the *Book of Documents*, a collection of rhetorical prose compiled by fourth century B.C.E., one of the Five Classics of ancient Chinese literature. The instrument was used to refer to kings and emperors of the world gathering together to practise and achieve integration of different tribes, countries and ethnic groups. This is today the core ideology of the Chinese nation as a multi-Minzu country. 协和万邦 can be used to refer to the fact that integration of different groups should be achieved through creating harmonious and unified alliances.

有容乃大—*Yǒu róng nǎi dà*
Can be translated as: *Tolerance is a virtue; accommodate others; a broad mind achieves greatness.*

有容 means that one has the capacity to assist others. 大 refers to great courage and an important cause. 容 (róng) means *to hold, to contain, to allow, to tolerate.* It is based on the two sub-characters of *roof, house* (which conveys the meaning) as well as *valley, ravine.*

有容乃大 is from the *Book of History*, a collection of poems from the Zhou Dynasty (eleventh to third centuries B.C.E.).

The word *tolerance* in English, which used to mean *endurance* and *fortitude*, is from Latin *tolerantia, a bearing, supporting, endurance*. The sense of tendency to be free from bigotry or severity in judging the other, is from the end of the eighteenth century.

Working Through the Principle of Harmony

Harmony is central to Chinese stories of interculturality (see Fig. 4.1). Although one can hear the word in other parts of the world to refer to human relations in and between countries, the word is not always put forward as a goal for interculturality. Other principles such as equality, social justice can be considered more important elsewhere. What harmony as a multifaceted notion signifies, deserves to be problematized further globally.

Fig. 4.1 The words 自由平等 (freedom and equality), 爱国 (patriotism), 富强 (prosperity), 和谐 (harmony), 文明和谐 (civilization and harmony) on a street panel in Chaoyang district (Beijing)

和谐—*Hé xié*
Can be translated as: *Harmony.*

和 (hé) is composed of 禾 (hé) *cereal, grain, rice, plant, stalk* and 口 (kǒu) for *mouth, entrance, gate, opening*. The second character behind harmony, 谐, means both *harmonious* and *humorous*. It is based on the merging of the characters for *words, speech* and *to speak* and, *all, every*, and *everybody.*

Harmony in Chinese describes a joint process of cooperation, coordination and friendship: 和, re: *together*; 协, xie: *cooperate*. The term originally referred to the combination of different tones in musical creations. It has also referred to peaceful coexistence regardless of differences and plurality (see Fig. 4.2). Harmony leads to not accepting violence and conflicts.

In English *harmony* was also first linked to music, especially in its Latin and Greek origins: *harmonia* referred to agreement and concord of sounds. The more concrete social meaning is from the fourteenth century.

以和为贵—*Yǐ hé wéi guì*
Can be translated as: *Harmony is the most precious; harmony is to be prized*

Fig. 4.2 A street sign containing the word 和 (harmony). Erdos, Inner Mongolia

为贵 (wéi guì) is based on 为 which indicates *strength, power, influence* and 贵 for *expensive, noble, precious*.

This discourse instrument is from the *Analects* (論語), a collection of the teachings and thoughts of the philosopher Confucius (551–479 BCE) with his students. It emphasizes the importance of harmony, as a joint process in human relations.

美美与共—*Měi měi yǔ gòng*
Can be translated as: *A diversified and harmonious world.*
Can also translate as: *Bring out the best in each other.*

美 (měi) refers to *beautiful, very satisfactory, good, to beautify* and *to be pleased with oneself*. Its ideographic is that of a person 大 wearing an elegant crown 羊. 共 (gòng) is the Chinese word for *common, general, to share, together, total, altogether*, whose ideographic is two hands holding one object.

This discourse instrument is from the *Book of Rites*: "各美其美, 美人之美；美美与共, 天下大同". This can translate as "Every form of beauty has its uniqueness, precious is to appreciate other forms of beauty with openness, if beauty represents itself with diversity and integrity, the world will be blessed with harmony and unity". This sentence has been reinvested by Chinese decision-makers in recent years to describe and promote 'glocal' interculturality, urging people to appreciate the culture of others as do to one's own, as a way of leading to harmony. It is also found in the phrase 美美与共, 天下大同, which can translate as "If they can coexist, there will be harmony in the world". This discourse instrument is also used as a slogan that can be seen for instance around the campus of Minzu University of China in Beijing (see Fig. 4.3), an interdisciplinary institution which focuses on Minzu 'ethnic' studies. It promotes the idea of tolerance between various people and groups, who are deemed to be "beautiful" in all their diversity.

君子和而不同，小人同而不和—*Jūn zǐ hé ér bù tóng, xiǎo rén tóng ér bù hé*
Can be translated as: *Gentlemen respect each other although they may disagree.*

君子 (jūnzǐ) is an important figure in Confucianism. Often translated in English as *the nobleperson, person of noble character*, the word is composed of 君 (jūn) for *monarch, lord, gentleperson, ruler*—ideographic: a leader giving orders—and 子 with a pictographic of a child in a wrap, with

Fig. 4.3 *A diversified and harmonious world.* Banner at the campus of Minzu University of China

outstretched arms but bundled legs. 同 (tóng) has an ideographic of sharing a common tongue. Finally, 不和 (bù hé) refers to *not to get along well, to be on bad terms, to be at odds*.

From the *Analects* of Confucius, the instrument can be translated as *one can be friendly to each other while disagreeing*; *gentlemen are in harmony but not in harmony*; but also, in a negative way as *villains are in harmony but not in harmony*. In brief: disagreement is allowed and can be the basis for friendliness, respect and harmony.

投桃报李—*Tóu táo bào lǐ*
Can be translated as: *Mutual courtesy*. As an idiom translates as: *Toss a peach, get back a plum*.

投 (tóu) means *to cast, to send, to throw oneself (e.g. into the river), to seek refuge, to place oneself into the hands of*. Its formation is based on a character for *hand* and another for *tool/weapon*. 桃 (táo) is *a peach*, 李 (lǐ) *a plum*. 报 (bào) refers to the English for *to announce, to inform, report, newspaper, recompense, revenge*. Its ideographic is a hand cuffing a criminal, sentencing them for a crime.

It is from the *Book of Songs*, one of the five Confucian classics containing poetry from ancient China. It refers to interchanging a gift as mutual courtesy: *When you give me an apple, I will also give you one in appreciation*. The principles of equality and mutual benefit are to be found behind this discourse tool. There are many phrases in the English language that seem to correspond to this discourse instrument: *to return a favour, to exchange gifts*, or *scratch my back, and I'll scratch yours*, although they do not always seem to connote the idea of building up the desire for long-lasting friendship in the process as this discourse instrument does. Equality in interculturality should involve long-term reciprocity and avoidance of benefice-seeking and profiteering from one side.

兼爱—*Jiān ài*
Can be translated as: *Universal love*.

兼 means *double, twice, simultaneous* and 爱, *love, affection*. 兼 (Jiān) has an ideographic of a hand holding two sheaves of grain and is found in Chinese words such as *to attend simultaneously to two or more things* and *to take over*. 爱 (ài)'s ideographic is that of bringing a friend into one's house.

In English, *universal* comes from Latin *universus* for *all together, whole* and *entire* and is connected to the word *universe*, itself from the adjective *universus* which literally meant *turned into one*. Love is based on Old English *lufu* which meant *feeling of love, affection*, but also *romantic sexual attraction*. To fall in love is from the sixteenth century.

兼爱 *universal love* (equal affection for all individuals), a concept of the Mohist School of thought (opposed to the principle of the Confucian school of *differentiated love*), is considered as the core of Mozi's social ethics. It asserts that people should love others as they love themselves.

四海—*Sìhǎi*
Can be translated as: *The four seas* or *the entire world*.

四 is *number four* in Chinese and has an ideographic of a child in a room with four walls. 海 is the *ocean* and *the sea* and can indicate *the presence of a great number of people* or *things*.

The discourse instrument refers to China in its entirety and/or to the entire world. In Ancient times, four seas bordered China: The East Sea, the South China Sea, the West Sea and the North Sea. 四海 can be used to mean *open-minded*, with many kinds of friends, and *cosmopolitan* (open to others, open to new experiences). The seas are thus here linked to going out to the other, and opening up to them.

十里不同俗—*Shílǐ bùtóng sú*
Can be translated as: *Other countries, other manners; ten miles is different.*

十 translates as *10*; 里 *a li* (an ancient Chinese measure of length, approximately 500 m), *interior, inside*; 不同 *different, not alike* and 俗 *custom, popular, vulgar*. 同 is *like, similar* and *together* and has an ideographic of sharing a common tongue.

This discourse instrument reminds us that another place has different characteristics that need to be borne in mind when visiting and interacting with the people in the other place or when meeting somewhere else. It calls for bearing in mind potential differences but also respecting them and acting accordingly. As a complement, we wish to remind our readers that something that appears different in the other might also be similar, or at least share some similitudes with what we already know.

各美其美，美人之美，美美与共，天下大同—*Gè měi qí měi, měirén zhīměi, měiměi yǔgòng, tiānxià dàtóng.*
Can be translated as: *Appreciate the culture/values of others as do to one's own, and the world will become a harmonious whole; everybody cherishes his or her own culture/values, and if we respect and treasure other's culture/values, the world will be a harmonious one (word-for-word translation: each has its own beauty, the beauty of the beauty, the beauty of the same, the world is the same).*

This discourse instrument was used by sociologist Fei Xiaotong (费孝通, 2015) in relation to Chinese Minzu (see Fig. 4.4).

In Chinese 美 (měi)—repeated six times in this instrument—means *beautiful, very satisfactory*, and *good*. Its ideographic is that of a person wearing an elegant crown. The character is also contained for example, in the words for *the United States* and *the fine arts* (painting). 天下 (Tiānxià) is translated as *the world* but refers to the fact that people are *all under the same sky* (天 = the sky).

Fig. 4.4 A biographical notice about Fei Xiaotong (费孝通) at Minzu University Museum

Although the key verbs of the English translation, *respect*, *cherish* and *treasure*, are implicit in the Chinese version, it is interesting to reflect on the etymology of these verbs. *To respect* comes from Latin *respectere* for *to look back at, regard* and *consider*. The idea of treating with differential esteem is from the end of the sixteenth century. *To cherish* is very much reminiscent of the French word *chérir*, from Latin *carus* for *dear, costly, beloved*, with roots in the idea of *to like, to desire*. Finally, *to treasure* is from both Latin *thesaurus, treasury, treasure* and Greek *thēsauros store, treasure, treasure house*.

All these verbs as well as the original Chinese remind us of the need to consider the other under a positive light and to accept and work upon our being together. 美美与共 hints at the idea of coexistence, togetherness of 'beauties' ('we are all in the same boat', in other words).

兼听—*Jiān tīng*

Can be translated as: *Listening to a variety of voices, to others; listening to opinions widely.*

兼 (jiān) can mean *double, twice, simultaneous* and 听 (tīng) *to listen, to hear*. 兼 has an ideographic of a hand holding two sheaves of grain and is found in Chinese words for expressing the idea of *annexing, acquiring, attending simultaneously to two or more things*. 听's ideographic is that of words reaching an ear.

This discourse instrument is central to interculturality. Be it when discussing one's views on life and relations or how we see interculturality ourselves, we must listen to others, and especially to as many voices as possible to enrich and open up our own way of thinking, our own worlds. The encounter/confrontation of ideas represents the only viable way to create *change* and thus interculturality between us. It is through the voices of others only that I can change and challenge myself with other opinions, ideas, worldviews.

道不同, 不相为谋—*Dào bùtóng, bù xiāng wéi móu*

Can be translated as: *Persons who walk different paths cannot make plans/work together.*

道 (dào) refers to *the road, the path*, and *the Dao of Daoism*. The meaning of the word is conveyed by the sub-character for *to walk*. The character 道 is contained in Chinese words for *to know, to become aware of, virtue, morality* and *ethics*. 相 (xiāng) has an ideographic of staring at a tree (i.e. observing) and means *each other, mutually*.

In English, an antonym for this discourse instrument could be *likeminded*. In order to 'do' interculturality, and thus trigger change in all those involved, one must negotiate, co-construct and share a common path *a minima*. This path must be based on a common understanding, which requires speaking to each other, identifying one's differences and similarities, power differentials and changing together, should those involved be willing to.

As a reminder *to change* in English comes from Late Latin *cambiare, to barter, exchange*, with an ancient root based on the words for *to bend, to crook*. One could say that interculturality occurs when those involved 'bend together' to come up jointly with a new idea, solution, worldview, and so on.

正名(辨正名称、名分，使名实相副)—*Zhèngmíng (biànzhèng míngchēng, míng fèn, shǐ míng shí xiāng fù)*

Can be translated as: *rectification of names; to replace the current name or title of something with a new one that reflects its true nature; to make a name match the reality.*

正 (zhèng) has an ideographic of a foot stopping in the right place. It can mean *straight, proper, principal, to rectify* and is found in Chinese words for *genuine, formal, official* (amongst others). 名 (míng) can mean *a name, a word, a place* and determine the attributes of a thing and its relations with other things. Its ideographic is a name called out to hail someone at night.

正名 reminds us that we need to be vigilant towards the words that we use when we speak with others and to rectify them when we realize that they might mean something else or have a different connotation/flavour. This endeavour is meaningful for example, when we translate words interculturally. One telling example is that of the use of the word *propaganda* in Chinese, English and most Indo-European languages whereby the connotation of this word varies immensely. As such, while in English and Indo-European languages the word refers to 'brainwashing', see even 'fake news', and is mostly pejorative, in Chinese the word also translates as *information, publicity* and does not have the same negative tone. It is interesting to note (interculturally speaking) that in the English language the word *propaganda* used to refer to a committee of representatives of the Catholic Church in charge of foreign missions.

Making Use of the Continuum of Difference and Similarity

The continuum of difference and similarity is very much present in many Chinese discourse instruments. This is a good opportunity for us to remember that interculturality should also lead us to balance these two aspects in order to allow change and transformation to take place between us (see Dervin, 2016, 2017).

合同异—*Hé tóng yì*
Can be translated as: *Unify/combine similarity and difference.*

同 means *contract.* 异 (yì) corresponds to the English words *different, other, hetero-, unusual, strange, surprising, to distinguish, to separate, to discriminate.* Its ideographic is that of a person 共 with a scary face 田. Put together these characters mean *same and different* (同异).

This discourse tool means that similarities and differences are relative. Looking at someone, a habit or a cultural artefact through the lenses of difference or similarity is always a viewpoint. There can be similarity in difference and difference in similarity. This is why both difference and similarity, as ideological and potentially judgemental elements of analysis, need to be considered systematically as an undividable pair. This discourse instrument is from the philosopher Hui Shi (380–305 B.C.E.).

大同而与小同异，此之谓 "小同异"。万物毕同毕异，此之谓"大同异"—*Dà tóng ér xiǎo tóng yì, cǐzhī wèi " xiǎo tóng yì". wàn wù bì tóng bì yì, cǐzhī wèi "dà tóng yì"*
Can be translated as: *Minor commonality and differentiation; similarity and small differences refer to roughly the same with slight differences.*

From Zhuangzi (庄子, 369–286 B.C.E.), one of the earliest texts to contribute to the philosophy known as Daojia (school of the Way): When things are totally identical or totally different, it is called major commonality and differentiation.

求同存异 hints at the idea that one should look for agreement while keeping one's values, seeking common ground while setting aside differences.

庄周梦蝶—*Zhuāng zhōu mèng dié*

Can be translated as: *Relative difference between all things is needed.*

蝶 (dié) is a butterfly.

From the *Zhuangzi*: Zhuangzi (庄子) dreams of a butterfly or is it the butterfly dreaming of Zhuangzi? This reminds us that there must be a difference between oneself and others, between all others, but that this is always relative. Things and people are changing, changeable, 'liquid' and the borders between them are not always so obvious.

For interculturality, this could entail keeping an eye on how we manage similarity and difference, keeping a potential short distance between us, while allowing co-change in terms of difference and similarity occurring between us.

道通为一—*Dào tōng wéi yī*

Can be translated as: *Opposite things complement each other.*

厉 (lai) used to mean *covered in scabs* in ancient Chinese.

From the Dao (Chinese for "way", "road", "path", "course", "speech", or "method") a fundamental concept of Chinese philosophy: beauty and ugliness are relative and are inherently the same. For the Dao different things in the universe are the same. Our opinions about what is *beautiful, clever, interesting, polite* is always relative and through engaging with other ways of seeing these elements, we can open our eyes to other values and realities, and thus avoid judgements which are not justified—and can potentially hurt others. It is not about pretending to change or to 'parrot' other discourses on these elements but to learn to shift between different worldviews, ideological positionings and to see one's own in different lights. We argue that this process only can open the door to a form of interculturality based on real change, that is, renegotiated, unthought and rethought change.

兵强则灭—*Bīng qiáng zé miè*

Can be translated as: *Everything has two sides;* word-for-word translation: *if the soldiers are strong, they will die.*

This discourse instrument derives from Laozi, the so-called founder of Taoism.

兵 (bīng) corresponds to the English words *soldiers, a force, an army* and *weapons*. Its ideographic is two hands 八 holding an axe 丘. 强 (qiáng) represents *a bow*, and the forms of *curved* and *arched*. 则 (zé) is a conjunction used to express contrast with a previous clause (e.g. but, then) and also refers *to standard, norm, principle, to imitate, to follow*. Its ideographic is that of laws inscribed 刂 on a slate 贝. Finally, 灭 (miè), in English means: *to extinguish* or *put out, to go out (of e.g. a fire), to exterminate* or *wipe out, to drown*. It has an ideographic of covering a flame. What the discourse instrument means is that strong soldiers will not always succeed if they are unable to balance between determination and care, strength and weakness.

兵强则灭 refers to the complexity of all things, hinting at the fact that everything is not unequivocal and that they can contain contradictions and incoherences (or what might appear as incoherent). Change might happen and turn a habit, an artefact, a word into something else. There is thus a need to be open to change, to the simplexity (simplicity + complexity, Dervin, 2016) of things, people, attitudes and discourses, to learn to balance the many and varied aspects of all those involved and to practice modesty in front of what appears to be different.

同归殊途—*Tóng guī shū tú*
Can be translated as: *Same destination but different routes; same goal, different ways.*

归 (guī) means *to return, to go back* and *to gather together*. Its ideographic is that of a wife returning home. 归根 (guī gēn) is the Chinese for *returning home after a lifetime's absence* or *to go back to one's roots*. 途 (tú) refers to *the way, route* and *road* in English and is based on the sub-characters for *walking* (which conveys the meaning) and *surplus, remainder*.

This discourse instrument reminds us that finding a solution to a problem requires exploring different alternatives, different ways of considering it. Different routes can lead to the same answer. Listening to how others try to solve problems, for example concerning equality and equity in relation to diversity in a specific society, might inspire us to look for other 'routes'.

见贤思齐焉，见不贤而内自省也—*Jiàn xián sī qí yān, jiàn bù xián ér nèi zìxǐng yě*
Can be translated as: *When one meets a virtuous person, one should consider learning from them; if one sees an immoral person, one should introspect to avoid being immoral.*

This discourse instrument is from *the Analects*.

自省 (zì xǐng) means to examine oneself critically/introspection, self-examination. 自 refers to *self, oneself* and has a pictographic of a nose (a symbol of self in China). 省 contains the sub-character for *few, little, less* and *eye, to look*, which conveys the meaning of the character. The word means *to inspect, to examine* and *to be aware*.

Introspection comes from the mirror effect of engaging, observing and interacting with others. What we see as 'good' and 'questionable' in others should help us reflect on our own ways, ideas, attitudes, and so on and experience transformations for and with others. The English word is from Latin *introspicere, to look into, to examine* and *to observe attentively*.

Learning with Each Other, Reciprocity in Interculturality

Interculturality requires cooperation, co-construction, some form of reciprocity and thus change, revising, unthinking together. Often this is formulated as learning from each other but we phrase it as learning with each other here (Li & Dervin, 2019)—transform self and other in a joint way. The following discourse instruments support us in reflecting on these processes.

教学相长—*Jiào xué xiāng zhǎng*
Can be translated as: *Teaching and learning promote each other.*

学 (xué) means *to learn, to study, to imitate,* but also *science*. The ideographic is that of a building 宀 where children 子 study. 长 (zhǎng) represents an old man with long hair and a cane. 相 has an ideographic of staring 目 at a tree 木 (i.e. to observe).

This discourse instrument urges us to see encounters as the double-bind of learning and teaching, both representing two sides of the same coin. In interculturality, we must open up to multifaceted learning and teaching, and being both the provider and receiver of these important processes. Teachers and students can improve each other; it is thus a two-way process. Interculturality is like teaching and learning; it represents the two interrelated sides of the same coin, each benefits from each other and can teach and learn with each other. This important idea hints at the need to avoid creating hierarchies between the one who is said to know and the one who does not know. We can learn from each other; teachers and students learn from each other. *Teaching is to learn, learning is to teach.* Interculturally we can all learn from and teach each other… teachers themselves should be open to learning from their students as far as interculturality is concerned, since, in many cases, they might have more intercultural experiences than teachers.

结拜—*Jié bài*
Can be translated as: *Sworn brothers or sisters.*

結 contains 纟 for *silk, thread* and 吉 for *lucky, propitious, good*. 拜 means *to pay respect, worship, visit* or *salute*. The radical 手 represents two hands put together in respect.

In some parts of China, one can have a 'godfather'/'godmother' for example from another of the 56 Minzu 'ethnic' groups of China, who can give one a boost by helping, coaching, supporting. By developing deep feelings and common goals amongst people who are not related by blood, one can develop brotherhood and sisterhood. Sworn brotherhood or sisterhood occurs thanks to a good relationship or a common purpose. Usually the sworn brother/sister has a good position in society and can support their protégé. Interculturally speaking this can also inspire us to develop strong and deep bonds with others.

相辅相成—*Xiāng fǔ xiāng chéng*
Can be translated as: *Supplement and complement each other.*

相 (xiāng) has the ideographic of to observe: to stare 目 at a tree 木. 辅 (fǔ) means *to assist, to complement* and is composed of sub-characters that refer to *a cart, a vehicle* and *to begin, man, father*. 成 (chéng) corresponds to: *to succeed, to finish, to complete, to accomplish, to become, to turn into, to be all right.*

相辅相成 refers to entities existing side by side and playing a part together; being inseparably interconnected and supplementary to each other.

知行合一—*Zhī xíng hé yī*

Can be translated as: *You learn something, you act upon it; knowledge and action should go hand in hand; knowledge is action, action is knowledge.*

知 (zhī) means *to know, to be aware* and is made up of components indicating *an arrow, a dart* but also *the mouth, entrance, gate* and *opening*. 行 (xíng) has an ideographic of taking small steps 亍 with one's feet 彳.

This discourse instrument put forward by a Ming Dynasty (1368–1644 A.D.) thinker is usually translated as *knowledge corresponds with action*. 知 (knowledge) includes 矢 *sound* and 口 *mouth*. What this means is that what you do should correspond to what you say and believe. *Discourses correspond to actions* (see Fig. 4.5). At the same time, the discourse instrument has a value meaning: 'stick to your words'. For interculturality, words and actions matter, especially when one thinks about discourse phenomena such as stereotypes, representations, misperceptions. If I use a generalization about myself (as in "we Finnish people do this or that!") I must take the responsibility of this assertion when I act or when people act around me in front of the Other, for example, by reflecting critically and openly about potential misleading statements that I might make. In a similar vein, while condemning or judging others for

Fig. 4.5 The discourse instrument of 知行合一 on a Chinese campus

what they do (or not), think (or not), deserves to be accompanied by us reflecting on our own actions to avoid hypocrisy and false modesty.

视人如己—*Shì rén rú jǐ*
Can be translated as: *Treat/see others as yourself.*

视 is *to look at, regard, inspect*; 人 *a man, a person*; 如 *as* and 己 *self, oneself*. 视 is based on sub-characters for *spirit* and *to see, observe* and *meet*. It is found in Chinese words for *to view as, to value* but also in the word for *television*. 己 has a pictographic of a loom woven with thread and contains a sub-character for *secret, hidden* and *mysterious*.

This discourse instrument is from Ge Hong's *The Baopuzi* (抱朴子, Master embracing simplicity), a Doaist treatise from the Jin period (265–420), and hints at the importance of sympathy and basic goodwill towards others.

礼尚往来—*Lǐshàngwǎnglái*
Can be translated as: *Reciprocity as a social norm, proper behaviour is based on reciprocity, to return politeness for politeness.* 投桃报李 (Tóutáobàolǐ— *to reciprocate*) is a synonym.

礼 (lǐ) is *the gift, rite, ceremony* in English. The sub-character of *spirit*, on which it is based, conveys its meaning. The character is found in the words for *gift, present, ceremony* and *etiquette* in Chinese. 尚 (shàng) is the Chinese for *to value, to esteem*. 往 (wǎng) for *to go, bound for, towards*, with the sub-character *to step with the left foot* conveying its meaning. Finally, 来 (lái) means *to come, to arrive, to come round* and has an ideographic of a wheat plant that has not yet borne fruit. It is found in words expressing *to come, to arrive, later, afterwards, more and more.*

Reciprocity is a discourse instrument from the *Book of Rites* which refers to etiquette in mutual communication. The *inter-* of interculturality refers to a never-ending process of in-betweenness, which should be complemented by reciprocity. The word reciprocity comes from Latin *reciprocare* which means *rise and fall, move back and forth*. Doing interculturality is moving back and forth ideas, identities, knowledge, ideologies, relations.

管鲍之交—*Guǎn bào zhī jiāo*
Can be translated as: *Friendship between Guan and Bao; as close as Guan Zhong and Bao Shuya; David and Jonathan.*

之 (zhī) is a possessive particle (*her, him, it*) while 交 (jiāo) translates as *to hand over, to turn over*, and *to make friends*. The latter has an ideographic of a person with crossed intersecting legs.

This discourse instrument describes a deep friendship based on strong mutual understanding. Guan Zhong (管) was an influential figure of the State of Qi in the Spring and Autumn Period (770–476 B.C.E.). He was close companion and business partner of Shuya (鲍). Guan Zhong and Bao Shuya represent paragons of friendship in China—like David and Jonathan in the Bible.

己所不欲，勿施于人—*Jǐ suǒ bù yù, wù shī yú rén*
Can be translated as: *Do unto others as you would have them do unto you; what you don't want done to you, don't do to others.*

己, which means self, oneself, has a pictographic of a loom woven with thread and contains a sub-character for *secret, hidden* and *mysterious*. 欲 (yú) translates as *desire, passion, to wish for, to desire*. The sub-character for *to lack, to owe, to breathe* conveys its meaning, while the other sub-character that composes it means *valley, gorge, ravine*. 施 (shī) means *to grant, to give, to act* and is composed of two sub-characters, one for *square, rectangle, region* and another for the former name of an indigenous tribe in South China.

This discourse instrument corresponds to the so-called Golden Rule, which is found in different documents from around the world. In China, it is from *the Analects*. In different global versions it can be formulated in positive or negative ways, for example, *Do as you would be done by others; do not do to others what you would not like to do.*

己所不欲，勿施于人 calls for us to reflect on what we do, why we do it in a certain, and the consequences of our actions for ourselves and others. By reflecting on our actions, and potentially revising them, we can treat and act towards others in different ways. This can also serve as a basis for reflecting together with other people.

三人行， 必有我师焉—*Sān rénxíng, bì yǒu wǒ shī*
Can be translated as: *When three people walk together, there must be someone worth imitating.*

师 (shī) is the Chinese word for *teacher, master, model*. Its ideographic represents to skilfully wield a knife and is composed of sub-characters for *a knife, to rotate* and *revolve*. 我 (wǒ) translates as *I, me, my*. Its ideographic is a hand holding a weapon.

This discourse instrument is from the *Analects* and refers to the idea that every single person has something we can find inspiration in—even those we might consider at first as *unworthy*. In the process, one should reflect on oneself: what characteristics can we change by looking at others (again: 'good' and 'bad')? Changing oneself and others is an important principle of interculturality. This instrument also reminds us that before judging others too quick, we might learn something from them.

Pause

This chapter focused on certain ways of thinking about and doing interculturality together. The polysemic term of *harmony* was often at the centre of attention, with *mutuality, differilitude* (difference-similitude) and '*beauty*' ('diversity') representing peripheral and yet essential components of interculturality. As we have seen while reviewing the instruments, these terms tend to be polysemic and we are urging our readers to negotiate their meanings and connotations again and again with their (intercultural) colleagues, interlocutors, partners, but also friends, family members. There is also a need to revise the preconceived ideas that we may have about some of these elements (e.g. harmony), which may not be part of our bread and butter of interculturality but which may 'hide' under other key-terms to which we might be more accustomed. Upon hearing these words, we need to refrain from judging (e.g. "how naïve!") and listen to how, why and by/for whom they are used. In other words, we need to build *reflexivity, tolerance* and *criticality* towards other ways of talking about interculturality in order to enrich our own 'vocabulary' to speak about such a complex notion. Making interculturality intercultural is listening carefully to other ways of engaging with the notion.

Figure 4.6 summarizes the main aspects contained in the chapter discourse instruments.

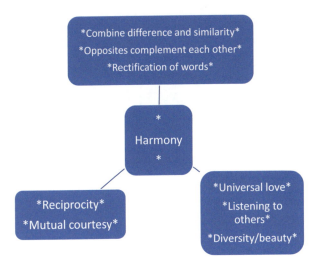

Fig. 4.6 Chapter summary

Thinking Further

- What does the idea of 'universal love' mean to you? What images come to your mind when you see/hear the phrase in English? Do you believe that such a thing as love can be 'universal'?
- How does the word *harmony* sound in the languages that you know? Is it a word that you use frequently to talk about relations, for example, in a family, an institution, a country?
- Which discourse instruments are used in your context (institutions, schools, companies) to hint at the need for harmony and other values relating to interculturality? Can you translate them into English?
- Do you find disagreement to be a 'healthy' part of interculturality? Have you found yourself in many intercultural situations where you have voiced your disagreement? What happened? Was it useful to disagree?

(*continued*)

(continued)

- Do people get trained to disagree in your context or is disagreement avoided, for example, in education?
- Try to find more information about this figure from Confucius' *Analects*: 君子 (jūnzǐ). What could be learnt for interculturality through acquainting ourselves with this 'gentle-person'?
- Do the idioms *to return a favor; to exchange gifts;* or *scratch my back, and I'll scratch yours,* in English and their equivalents in other languages connote the idea of building up the desire for long-lasting friendship?
- What do you make of the idea of loving others as you love yourself? What does this mean concretely to you?
- Try to find out some information about scholar Fei Xiaotong (费孝通). Can you identify some of his writings in English and other languages? What appear to be his strongest ideas for thinking about interculturality?
- 天下 (Tiānxià) has been an important discourse instrument used in China to think about the world in the past and increasingly today. What kind of information can you find about it?
- 兼听—*Jiān tīng* is a central aspect of interculturality. Is this something that you systematically pay attention to? Listening to different voices, giving the floor to others and making sure your own voice is also heard? What strategies do you use to do so?
- Why do you think of the idea that 'persons who walk different paths cannot make plans/work together'? Do you fully agree with this discourse instrument?
- If you think of 正名 (rectification of names), list words, concepts, notions used in English and/or other languages to discuss interculturality that you would like to 'rectify'. Explain why.
- Choose a word that you think has a different flavour in English and other languages and do an 'archaeology' of the word in the languages that you know: where does it come from? How has its meaning evolved during the centuries? (See the example of *propaganda* in Chinese vs. English which has a completely different connotation).

(*continued*)

(continued)

- Can you think of an example of you learning something new while considering how 'opposite things complement each other'?
- Have you ever been in a situation where someone thought about, behaved or found a solution for a problem that was very different from how you would do it—although it worked well? Can you describe this situation and explain how you would have solved the same problem and why? Who/what would influence you in doing it in another way?
- Do you think that your (current/former) teachers have learnt anything from you? Explain.
- What would you say would be the most important thing to learn with other countries at the moment *versus learn from*? Take a concrete context and reflect.
- During the course of a day, try to observe how often you try to see others as yourself—or not—and for what purposes. What do you notice?
- In how many of the encounters and relations you experience every day do you do 'reciprocity'? With whom, how and why?
- Change is omnipresent in the discourse instruments that we have explored hitherto. The philosopher Georg Lichtenberg (2012: 128) writes about change: "I cannot say whether things will get better if we change; what I can say is that they must change if they are to get better". Do you really see change as central to 'doing' interculturality at this stage? Do you agree with Lichtenberg that 'change must happen'?
- Do you agree that we can learn with/from any single person? Again, for one day, jot down all the types of learning that you experience with every person you meet (from your best friend to a street cleaner). What do you notice? Why does reflecting on this matter? How does it connect potentially to interculturality?

(*continued*)

(continued)

- When asked to identify a Chinese discourse instrument, a student proposed this one and explained it this way: "The attitude of 'seeing is believing' (眼见为实) is significant, since the understanding of other cultures should be based on multiple sources of information and first-hand experience, avoiding gazing at and constructing other civilizations in imagination, such as orientalism." Do you know a similar discourse instrument in any of the languages that you know? What does it mean to you? Do you think that witnessing, 'seeing', something or someone, can really help us approach them from a more 'authentic' way?

References

Abdallah-Pretceille, M. (2006). Interculturalism as a Paradigm for Thinking About Diversity. *Intercultural Education, 17*(5), 475–483.

Dervin, F. (2016). *Interculturality in Education: A Theoretical and Methodological Toolbox*. Palgrave Macmillan.

Dervin, F. (2017). *Critical Interculturality: Lectures and Notes*. Cambridge Scholars Publishing.

Fei, X. (2015). *Globalization and Cultural Self-Awareness*. Springer.

Ferri, G. (2018). *Intercultural Communication: Critical Approaches, Future Challenges*. Palgrave Macmillan.

Kool, V. K., & Agrawal, R. (2020). *Gandhi and the Psychology of Nonviolence*. Palgrave Macmillan.

Li, Y., & Dervin, F. (2019). *Continuing Professional Development of Teachers in Finland*. Palgrave Macmillan.

Lichtenberg, G. C. (2012). *Philosophical Writings*. State University of New York Press.

Piller, I. (2010). *Intercultural Communication: A Critical Introduction*. Edinburgh University Press.

CHAPTER 5

Making Interculturality Work Together, as Group/Community Members

INTRODUCTION

Togetherness, groupness and *community* are polysemic keywords found in all kinds of discourses today to refer to 'us', 'them'; 'identity', 'solidarity' but also (randomly) 'conflict', 'home' and so on (see e.g. Bauman, 2000; Sutherland, 2017). Take the word *community* for example, which was not necessarily used much in many parts of the world even ten years ago; it now seems to be ubiquitous in English and in different languages (community shares the same etymology as the word *common* in English). Like togetherness and groupness, community appears to be a 'butterfly' term, which flaps its wings in all directions. What we make of these words in English and other languages when we talk about interculturality deserves to be reflected upon.

Politics, education, marketing, (social) media, all make use of these key terms to create specific sentiments for example, of belonging to a narrow/broad group and to infuse ways of thinking in each and every one of us around the globe.

In interculturality, these three keywords can be said to be crucial since it is through our identification with them that we meet the other, identify for, with and against them and accept and experience change. In this

© The Author(s), under exclusive license to Springer Nature Switzerland AG 2022
M. Yuan et al., *Change and Exchange in Global Education*, Palgrave Studies on Chinese Education in a Global Perspective,
https://doi.org/10.1007/978-3-031-12770-0_5

chapter, we explore Chinese instruments that can allow those interested in interculturality as bonding, coming together and identifying with a group/groups, to reflect further on this important aspect, especially in relation to belonging and differilitude.

This chapter revolves around the following sections: Chinese Political Initiatives Related to Interculturality, Reflecting on What Togetherness Entails Within the Context of Chinese Minzu, Reflecting on Togetherness and Interculturality from a more Global Perspective, The Objectives and Benefits of Togetherness, Learning Togetherness.

CHINESE POLITICAL INITIATIVES RELATED TO INTERCULTURALITY

In this first section, we focus on discourse instruments that introduce current Chinese ideologies of togetherness, inwards and outwards.

民族—*Mín zú*

Can be translated as: *Ethnic (group), nation(ality), Minzu (preferred).*

民 (mín) has the words *the people, nationality* and *citizen* as equivalents in English. Its ideographic is that of an eye pierced by a dagger (a symbol of slavery in the past). In Chinese, the character is found in words expressing *the people, farmers, residents* and *democracy*. 族 (zú) translates as *race, ethnicity, nationality* and *clan*. Its ideographic is symbolic of a group of people who swear by a single flag (方 is a flag). 族 composes words such as *the Chinese people, family* and *ethnic groups*.

The use of the word 民族 was inspired by Japanese (minzoku, みんぞく) in the late nineteenth century, making the notion part of the discourse on Chinese nation building.

In English, 民族 is often (mis-)translated as *nationality/nation* to refer to the different Minzu groups that compose China. The word *nation* in English used to refer to a large group of people with common ancestry and language and is from Latin *nationem* for *birth, origin, race of people, tribe*, with an emphasis on giving birth, begetting. The ideas of nation-building and nation-state date back to the early twentieth century in English.

In Chinese 民族 (Mín zú) refers to an established community formed through long-term historical development and bonds, distinguished by specific characteristics (e.g. language) from other groups. A single country can have different 民族 too, as is the case of China, which is a unitary multi-ethnic country. As such, 56 Minzu groups constitute today's Mainland China, for example, they include the Han, Hui, Mongolian, Uygur, Zhuang. Different Minzu groups are located in different parts of China, with many on the borders with other countries. At the age of 18, Chinese citizens may change their 民族 following the one of their father or mother. Minzu groups share similarities and differences in terms for example, of culture, language, worldview (see Fig. 5.1). We note that other regions of China such as Hong Kong do not classify their residents using the same Minzu categories.

民族团结—*Mín zú tuán jié*
Can be translated as: *National unity, ethnic solidarity, ethnic harmony.*

团 (tuán) refers to *round, to roll into a ball, to gather* in English and has an ideographic of a lot of talent gathered in one place. The character is found in the words for *solidarity, corporation* and *organization* in Chinese.

Fig. 5.1 The innovation and entrepreneurship centre of Minzu University of China, with the logo 56 创 (to create/entrepreneurship) in reference to the 56 Minzu groups of China

结 (jié) has the sub-character for *thread, silk* at the core of its meaning. It translates as *a knot, a bond, a tie* and it is found in the words *to unite, to conclude* in Chinese.

民族团结 symbolizes solidarity between Chinese Minzu people (see Fig. 5.2). As indicated in the fourth article of the Constitution of the People's Republic of China (1982), "All ethnic groups in the People's Republic of China are equal." Equality, solidarity and mutual assistance among all Minzu groups are guaranteed by the Constitution, which means that discrimination and oppression are prohibited. Minzu unity goes hand in hand with the important aspect of prosperity and development. In the 'West', the ideas of *social justice* and *equality/equity*, found in research, education and policy-making overlap with many aspects of 民族团结. Finally, the idea of *unity* is also found in many other nations, for example, in the names of some countries such as the *United* Arab Emirates, the *United* States, the *United* Kingdom and serves as a national value, for

Fig. 5.2 Commemorative stamps for Minzu University of China, celebrating the 'Great Unity of the Chinese Nation'

example, every November 4 since 1861 Italy celebrates its *National Unity and Armed Forces Day*.

中华民族多元一体化—*Zhōng huá mín zú duō yuán yī tǐ huà*
Can be translated as: *plural unity pattern; pluralistic unity; the Chinese nation is pluralistic and unified*.

中华民族 refers to *the Chinese people*; 多元 translates as *poly-, multi-* and 一体化 as *integration, incorporation, unification*.
中 is the character for *middle, centre*, but also *China* and *Chinese*. Its ideographic is that of a line through the centre of a box. 华 represents here an abbreviation for China and it also means *magnificent, splendid* and *flowery*. 一 means *one, single* but also *whole*. Its ideographic represents *heaven, earth*, or the number 1. The character is found in Chinese words for *a little, same, equal, everything*. 体 is *the body, style, substance* and is based on sub-characters for *man, person* and *root, origin*. The last character of the discourse instrument is 化 for *change* found in words like *culture, civilization, modernization*.
One comment about the word *unity* in English here: It comes from Latin *unitatem* for *oneness, sameness* and *agreement* (*unus = one*).
What the discourse instrument, translated as *The Chinese nation's pluralistic unity pattern*, and based on a theory by the aforementioned sociologist Fei Xiaotong (2015), refers to is the necessity to think in terms of both plurality and unity when considering the relations and identifications of the diverse individuals who compose a national indivisible entity like China. This requires considering both differences and what connects people in a cohesive and non-contradictory way.

中华民族共同体意识—*Zhōng huá mín zú gòng tóng tǐ yì shí*
Can be translated as: *The sense of community of the Chinese nation*.

中华民族 translates as *the Chinese people*. 共同体 is *community* in English. 意识 means *consciousness, awareness*.
共 (gong) is *common, general, to share* and *altogether* (but also *the Communist Party*). Its ideographic is two hands holding one object. 同 (tóng) has the ideographic of sharing a common tongue and means *like, same, similar*. 体 (tǐ) is *the body, form, style* and *system*, containing the radical for a person. Consciousness and awareness are composed of 意 (yì) for *idea, meaning, thought* and *intention*, with the Chinese character for heart

conveying its meaning. 识 (shí) refers to *knowledge* and contains a sub-character for *speech, words*.

In English, the word *community* is from Latin *communitatem* for *community, society, fellowship, courtesy* and is based on the adjective *communis* for *common, public, general, shared by all or many*. The current meaning of the word is from the fifteenth century.

This discourse instrument links directly to the idea of the "Chinese Dream for all Chinese Minzu", shared interests, common development and values (e.g. a shared identity). It was advocated by Chinese President Xi Jinping at the Central Conference on Ethnic Affairs in September 2014. Minzu is seen as an important feature of Mainland China and a favourable one for development, different Minzu cultures represent an important part of Chinese culture as a whole and should be considered as such. 中华民族共同体意识 requires members of different Minzu groups to not only identify with their community but also with the entire Chinese nation, in order to balance diversity and unity.

优惠政策—*Yōu huì zhèng cè*
Can be translated as: *Preferential policies*.

优惠 means *privilege, discount* and *preferential*; 政策 refers to *policies*. 优 (Yōu) translates as *excellent, superior* and is based on the sub-character of *a person*, which conveys its meaning. It is found in words expressing *excellent, superiority, first-rate* in Chinese. 惠 (huì) has the following equivalents in English: *favour, benefit* and it is based on the sub-character for *heart*. It is used in words for *privilege, advantageous*, but also *mutual benefit* and *reciprocal*. 政 (zhèng) simply means *political, politics* and *government* and is based on the sub-character for *script*, which conveys its meaning. To finish, 策 (cè) refers to *policy, plan*, but also to *the bamboo slips* that were used for writing in Ancient China. It is based on the sub-character for *bamboo* and *flute*.

In China, there are many preferential policies for Minzu 'minority' groups: Regional Minzu autonomy (155 autonomous areas: regions, prefectures and banners); the right to give birth to children is not limited the same way as it is for Han majority people; getting extra points in college entrance examinations and postgraduate entrance examinations; big companies must have a certain proportion of Minzu workers.

一带一路—*Yī dài yī lù*
Can be translated as: *One Belt One Road.*

带 (dài) is a Chinese word for: *band, ribbon, belt* but also *area* and *zone*. Its ideographic is that of a belt, creasing one's robe above but not below. The character is found in words used to express *to guide, to lead, to take the lead, to set an example.* 路 (lù) means *journey, route* and *line* and is based on a sub-character for *foot, to satisfy, enough.*

一带一路 is a discourse instrument representing China's current main supra-national paradigm, a new model for global cooperation. Initiated in 2013 One Belt One Road is inspired by past global initiatives which are often referred to as the *Silk Road(s)*. Economically, it is meant to lead to the implementation of a free trade zone with neighbouring countries and building regional economic integration. In 2021, 140 countries and 32 international organizations have signed cooperation documents with China within the framework of this initiative. The principles of common consultation, joint contribution and shared benefits are central to the idea of the Belt and Road. 一带一路 also promotes reciprocal learning, mutual respect, openness and peace. The discourse instrument of a *community with a shared future for mankind*, which is central to the Belt and Road initiative has a direct link to interculturality.

人类命运共同体—*Rén lèi mìng yùn gòng tóng tǐ*
Can be translated as: *A community with a shared future for mankind.*

This instrument relies on three sets of characters: 人类 (rén lèi) for *human, humanity, mankind*; 命运 (mìng yùn) for *fate* and *destiny*; 共同体 (gòng tóng tǐ) for *community*.

人 is the character for *a person/people* and has a pictographic of the legs of a human being. 类 is used to refer to *a kind, type, category*, with the sub-character for *rice, millet* at its core. 命 is the equivalent for *life, fate, order* or *command* in English, with an ideographic showing an order given by mouth. The character is used in words for *revolution, a mission* and *a task to which one devotes oneself.* 运 can mean *to move, to transport, to use* or *apply*, with the sub-character for *to walk* conveying its meaning. 共 translates as c*ommon, general, to share, together* in English. It has an ideographic of two hands holding one object. The last two characters of the word *community* include 同 for *like, same, similar, together*, with an ideographic of sharing a common tongue and 体 for *body, style, substance*—with the sub-character for *a person* at its core.

This discourse instrument was presented by President Xi Jinping in Geneva, Switzerland in 2017. It epitomizes China's answer to the challenges and problems facing the world. Multipolarity, development, economic globalization, sustainable development, peace, cooperation and win-win outcomes are the keywords of 人类命运共同体.

上海精神—*Shànghǎi jīngshén*
Can be translated as: *Shanghai spirit*.

The instrument is based on two sets of characters: 上海, which refers to the *Chinese city Shànghǎi* and 精神 (jīngshén) for *spirit, mind, consciousness*. 精 is *essence, extract, energy*, with *grain, rice* as a sub-character conveying the meaning; 神 is the character for *deity, soul, spirit* and *mysterious*.

The Shanghai spirit is linked to the Shanghai Cooperation Organization (set up in 2001) and is based on a set of values approved of by the members of the Organization (e.g. India, Kazakhstan, Pakistan). The activities of the Organization rely on cooperation in economy, people-to-people exchanges, politics, security, and so on. The values include consultation, equality, joint development, mutual benefit, mutual trust and respect.

Reflecting on What Togetherness Entails Within the Context of Chinese Minzu

石榴同心—*Shí liu tóng xīn*
Can be translated as: *United closely as seeds of a pomegranate*.

石榴 is a chambered, many-seeded fruit called *pomegranate* and is composed of 石 (ideographic of a rock at the base of a cliff) and 榴 (*pomegranate*), with the sub-character for a tree conveying its meaning. 同心 translates as *to be of one mind, united*. 同 means *like, same, similar* and *together* and has an ideographic of sharing a common tongue. 心 is *the heart, mind* and *centre* in English and has a pictographic of a heart. It is used in words for *psychology, mentality, mood*, and also *anxious, uneasy* in Chinese.

In the English language the pomegranate comes from Latin *granata* for *grain* (*pomum granatum* meant literally *apple with many seeds*).

The discourse instrument is based on a metaphor (*united like pomegranate seeds*) used by President Xi Jinping to refer to the 56 Minzu groups of China, and their endeavour to support each other to improve their economic status, livelihood and to achieve development and prosperity.

大杂居小聚居—*Dà zá jū xiǎo jù jū*

Can be translated as: *Minzu groups live with each other, while some live in concentrated communities; (word-for-word translation:) large mixed living and small living together.*

大 means *big, major, great, wide* (ideographic: a man with outstretched arms). 杂居 refers to *cohabitation of different populations* and *coexistence*. 小 translates as *small, tiny, young*. 聚居 is *to inhabit a region* (esp. a Minzu area). 杂 (zá) can mean *mixed, various* and has the radical of a tree. 居 (jū), for which the character for *door* conveys the meaning, means *to reside, to store up* while 聚 (jù) translates as *to congregate, to assemble, to mass*, with an ideographic for people standing side-by-side, hand-to-ear.

In the English language, the idea behind the adverb *together* comes from Old English *togædere* meaning *so as to be present in one place, in a group, in an accumulated mass*.

This discourse instrument refers to the fact that different Minzu groups live together and mix, leading to many examples of mutual exchanges, cooperation and unity. They may live in large or small areas together (e.g. a border place in Xinjiang, a big metropolis like Shanghai). Encounters and coexistence may trigger a better sense of togetherness.

一体多元—*Yī tǐ duō yuán*

Can translate as: *United but pluralistic; (word-for-word translation:) 'one multi-dimensional'.*

一 means *one* in Chinese. 一体 refers to *an integral whole, all concerned and/or everybody*; 多元 is the word for *poly-, multi-*. 体 (tǐ) refers to *the body, form, substance* and includes the radical for *person* in Chinese. 多 (duō) is the word for *many, a lot of, numerous*, with an ideographic for two nights (i.e. *many*). 元 (yuan) translates as *first, original, a part of*, with a pictographic of a man with two lines emphasizing their head.

This discourse instrument works hand in hand with many other such instruments that refer to the importance of taking into account diversity and unity of various Minzu groups in China, while bearing in mind inclusion, exchanges, economic interdependence and emotional closeness and togetherness. Modernization, well-being and yearning for a better life represent the ultimate goals of 一体多元. In the 'West', this might be discussed in terms of social justice, equality and equity.

民族情怀—*Mín zú qíng huái*
Can be translated as: *Minzu feelings/sentiments; the passion and beloved feelings for all Minzu groups in China.*

情怀 is the Chinese for *feelings* and *mood*. 情 (qíng), which contains the sub-character for heart conveying its meaning, translates as *feeling, emotion* and *passion*. 怀 (huái) designates the *heart, bosom, mind* and for example, *to conceive a child*. The word also contains heart as a sub-character.

民族情怀 refers to positive feelings of togetherness and vitality in relation to the Chinese nation. This discourse instrument goes hand in hand with the idea of the *Chinese Dream*, which puts forward prosperity, rejuvenation and happiness of the people. The values of equality, self-respect, happiness, freedom, safety and development are connected to the Chinese dream too (see Fig. 5.3).

精神相依—*Jīng shén xiāng yī*
Can be translated as: *People from Minzu groups rely on each other's spirit; (word-for-word translation:) spiritual interdependence.*

This discourse instrument is composed of two sets of characters: 精神 for *spirit, mind, consciousness* and 相依 for *to be interdependent*. 精 (Jīng) translates as *essence, vitality, ability* (amongst others) and has a grain as a sub-character conveying its meaning. 神 (shén) refers to *a deity, the soul, spirit* and is used to express the fact that *something/someone is unusual, mysterious*. The sub-character for *spirit* conveys its meaning. 相 (xiāng) has the ideographic of to stare at a tree (i.e. to observe), and means *each other, mutually*. Finally, 依 (yī) is equivalent to the verbs *to depend on, to comply with* or *listen to somebody*. It contains the sub-character of *a person*, which conveys the meaning of the character.

This discourse instrument calls for reciprocity and mutuality, especially in terms of spirit, and attitude but also determination, in Minzu relations. Through interdependence, cooperation, open-mindedness Minzu groups can thrive and build a stronger sense of togetherness and unity.

Fig. 5.3 The words *Happy* and *Happiness* are often seen or heard in Chinese and/or English in China, as is the case here on a street vendor car

Reflecting on Togetherness and Interculturality from a More Global Perspective

天下乃天下之天下—*Tiānxià nǎi tiānxià zhī tiānxià*
Can be translated as: *The world is the world of the world; all under heaven belongs to the people.*

Three sets of characters compose this instrument: 天下 (Tiānxià, repeated three times), which means *land under heaven, the whole world* or *the whole of China*; 乃 (nǎi, with an ideographic of a pregnant woman) for *to be* but also *so, therefore* and *then*; 之 (zhī, ideographic of a foot suggesting that one should follow someone/something) is a possessive particle, it can mean *him, her, it* too.

This discourse instrument contains the important and recurring idea of 天下 (Tiānxià), *all under heaven*. What the instrument means is that a country does not belong to one person (e.g. a ruler) but to the people, and that, if a ruler acts immorally or unjustly, they cannot continue to rule and thus be replaced. If one uses an anachronic term from today, we could say that this discourse instrument of interculturality call for human rights to be respected by those in power. In 2021, The University of California Press published an important translation of a book by the philosopher Tingyang Zhao (2021) entitled *All under Heaven: The Tianxia System for a Possible World Order*, where the concept of 天下 is introduced.

海内存知己, 天涯诺比邻—*Hǎi nèi cún zhī jǐ, tiān yá ruò bǐ lín*
Can be translated as: *The sea is an intimate friend/a confident; the world is close by.*

海 refers to *the ocean/the sea*; 知己 to *an intimate friend, a confident* but also *to know oneself*; 天涯 is *a faraway place* or *the other end of the world*; 诺, *to consent, to promise*; 比邻 is *a neighbour* but also *near/next to*. The word for *ocean* and *sea* (海) is also found in the Chinese words for *overseas, abroad* and *border crossing inspection*. 内 translates as *inside, inner*, and has an ideographic of a man entering a door. It is found in words for *domestic, the innermost being*. 存 is linked to the ideas of *existing, storing, keeping* and *surviving* and contains the sub-character for *a son, child, seed* and *egg*, conveying its meaning. 知 is *to know* and *to be aware*, with the sub-character for *mouth, entrance* and *gate* conveying its main meaning. The character is found in words that express *knowledge, finding out, informing*. 己's pictographic is that of a loom woven with a thread and refers to *self, oneself*. 天 is the *sky* or *heaven*, with an ideographic of the heavens above a man. 涯 is *the border, the horizon, the shore* and contains the sub-character for *water* which conveys the meaning. It is contained in words for *career, period of one's life, separated worlds apart*. 诺 translates as *to consent, to promise* and has the sub-character for *words, speech* and *to say* conveying its meaning. The final two characters of the discourse instrument are: 比 for *to compare, to gesture*, with an ideographic of two spoons side-by-side and 邻 for *the neighbour, adjacent, close to*, with the sub-character for *place, town, city* conveying its meaning.

This discourse instrument describes the connection of thoughts and feelings taking place even if people are far away from each other. Derived from a poem by Wang Bo (王勃, 649–676 A.D.), the instrument relates to farewell and to not be sad when one is parting with friends. It reminds us that distance does not necessarily mean we cannot be friends.

唇亡齿寒—*Chúnwángchǐhán*

Can be translated as: *Lips and teeth are cold; once the lips are gone, the teeth will feel cold; intimately interdependent; close partners.*

唇 (chún) refers directly to *the lips* and is composed of a sub-character for *the mouth*. It is found in for example, the verbs *to retort, to answer back sarcastically*. 亡 (wáng) translates as *to die, to lose, to be gone* and has an ideographic of a man in a coffin. This character is used in words to express *death, casualties, to be destroyed*. 齿 (chǐ) is *the tooth*, with a sub-character for *to stop, to halt*. 寒 (hán) refers to *cold, poor, to tremble*, with a sub-character for *a house roof*.

唇亡齿寒 indicates that one should seek amity with neighbours and that interdependence is needed to support each other. It also hints at the idea that one should think long-term rather than try to reap benefits immediately. Looking at things from a broader perspective, examining and reflecting on the links between people, things, situations are also 'good practices' for close and reliable partnerships. *Why are we together? What is the basis of our cooperation? What are the expected outcomes for both of us? Do we have a hidden agenda that would need to be disclosed to make the relationship more transparent?*

你中有我，我中有你—*Nǐ zhōng yǒu wǒ, wǒ zhōng yǒu nǐ*

Can be translated as: *You have me, I have you; there is me in you and you in me.*

Four different characters, repeated several times are used in this discourse instrument: 你 (nǐ, with an ideographic of a pronoun for a person) for *you*; 中 (zhōng, ideographic: a line through the centre of a box) for *middle, centre, China/Chinese*; 有 (yǒu, with the radical of the moon) for *to have, to be, to exist*; 我 (wǒ, ideographic: a hand holding a weapon) for *I, me, my*.

This discourse instrument, like many others, refers to the importance of taking into account both interconnection and reciprocity. A hint at a community and a future where everyone has a stake, where everyone is bound to each other, is also present in 你中有我，我中有你.

求大同存小异—*Qiú dàtóng cún xiǎo yì*

Can be translated as: *Seek common ground while reserving differences; seek common ground and small differences.*

The instrument is composed of: 求 (qiú, found also in the idiom *to seek truth from facts*, that is, to be practical and realistic in Chinese) for *to seek, to look for, to demand*; 大同 (dàtóng, 大 means *big*, 同 *like, similar, together*) for *Great Harmony* (a Confucian concept for an ideal society); 存 (cún, with the sub-character for *seed* conveying its meaning) for *to exist, to deposit, to store*; 小 (xiǎo, with an ideographic of dividing by a line) for *small, tiny, few, young*; 异 (yì, with a simplified ideographic of another character for a person with a scary face) for *different, other, unusual, strange* (amongst others).

This discourse instrument appears central for interculturality: we will definitely always find ways of disagreeing with each other, however, in order to be and change together (i.e. 大同, *Great Harmony*) we must also seek commonalities. If the common ground is basic, differences do not necessarily become burdens. This way we can get closer to each other, engage in deep and meaningful interaction and be with each other in a more tolerant and respectful way. 求大同存小异 is central to for example, the discourse instrument of a community with a shared future for mankind discussed earlier.

OBJECTIVES AND BENEFITS OF TOGETHERNESS

手足情深—*Shǒu zú qíng shēn*

Can be translated as: *People get along very well like Castor and Pollux* (figures of semi-divine twins and patrons in Greek and Roman mythologies); *the love between brothers is deep; brotherhood.*

手 (shǒu) is *hand, to hold, convenient* and has a pictographic of a hand with the fingers splayed; 足 (zú, pictographic: the leg above the foot) refers to *foot, to be sufficient, ample*; 情 (qíng) means *feeling, emotion, passion*, with the sub-character of the heart conveying its meaning; 深 (shēn) translates as *deep, depth, rich* and has an ideographic of deep water.

This discourse instrument refers to the deep feelings that one can develop with and for others (and vice versa). The Chinese contains words for hand and foot to highlight such 'brotherhood'.

亲诚惠容—*Qīn chéng huì róng*
Can be translated as: *Sincerely welcome; inclusiveness.*

The discourse instrument is based on the combination of four characters: 亲 (qīn, ideographic: a tree bearing fruit) for *parent, relative, intimate* (character found in the words for *mother, father* too); 诚 (chéng, with the radical for *words, speech*) for *sincere, authentic*; 惠 (huì, with the sub-character for *heart* conveying its meaning) for *favour, benefit, to bestow*; and 容 (róng, with the sub-character for *the roof* conveying its meaning) for *to hold, to contain, to tolerate.*

This discourse instrument refers to kindness, sincerity, equality and tolerance in relations with other, with an aim to open up to the other and create peaceful interactions. 亲诚惠容 has also been used by Chinese decision-makers as a diplomatic concept.

人心归聚—*Rén xīn jù guī*
Can be translated as: *People come together.*

This instrument revolves around three sets of characters: 人心 (rén xīn) for *a popular feeling* and *the will of the people*; 归 (jù, ideographic of a simplified form for a wife returning home) for *to return, to give back to, to be taken care of by* and 聚 (guī, ideographic: people standing side-by-side, hand-to-ear) for *to congregate, to assemble, to amass.*

人心归聚 represents another discourse instrument for interculturality that calls for people to create a sense of unity and togetherness by being caring, tolerant and open-minded. This instrument has to do with Chinese Minzu unity.

怀远以德—*Huái yuǎn yǐ dé*
Can be translated as: *Embrace/respect distant peoples by means of virtue.*

怀 is the *bosom, heart, mind* and *to harbour in one's mind* in English. It contains the sub-character for *heart* and is used in words such as *to be sceptical of, to cherish the memory of* and *feelings/mood*. 远 is *far, distant, remote* and has the sub-character for *walking* conveying its meaning. 以 translates as *to use*, but also *by means of, according to* and has the character for *person* as a radical. 德 refers to *virtue, goodness, ethics* and contains the character for *heart*, which conveys its meaning.

This instrument hints at the necessity to offer special and altruistic policies for different groups, especially in secluded areas, in order to be able to create bonds, unity and a sense of togetherness. It also calls for individuals to reach out to other people by making efforts to meet them.

守望相助—*Shǒu wàng xiāng zhù*
Can be translated as: *To keep watch and defend one another; to join forces to defend against external aggressors; mutual help and protection.*

守 (shǒu) means *to guard, to defend, to keep watch* but also *to abide by the law*. It has an ideographic of keeping something within one's walls. 望 (wàng) is *the full moon*, but also *to hope, to expect, to look towards*. Its ideographic is that of a king gazing at the moon. 相 (xiāng) has an ideographic of to stare at a tree (i.e. to observe) and refers to *each other, mutually*. The last character, 助 (zhù), means *to help* and has the sub-character of *power, strength*, conveying its meaning.

This discourse instrument is from Mencius. Although it might sound bellicose, 守望相助 can help us reflect on how to cooperate and support each other in times of crisis by giving a helping hand and supporting each other for example, interculturally.

吸收外国文化有益成果—*Xī shōu wài guó wén huà yǒu yì chéng guǒ*
Can be translated as: *Absorbing the good sides of foreign cultures.*

The discourse instrument is based on five sets of characters: 吸收 (xī shōu) *to absorb, to assimilate*; 外国 (wài guó) for *foreign country*; 文化 (wén huà) for *culture, civilization*; 有益 (yǒu yì) for *useful, beneficial* and 成果 (chéng guǒ) for *result, achievement, profit*. 吸 refers to *breathe, suck in* and *absorb* and has mouth as a sub-character conveying its meaning. 收 means *to receive, to accept* and *to collect*, with the sub-character of *the hand* conveying its meaning. 外 is the Chinese character for *outside, foreign* and *external*. Its ideographic is night-time divinations (the supernatural, the foreign). 国 can be translated as *country, nation* and *state*. Its ideographic is that of a treasure within a country's borders. 有 is the character for *to have, to exist* and *to be*, with the moon as a sub-character conveying its meaning. 益 translates as *benefit, profit* and *advantage*. Its ideographic is that of a container overflowing with water. 成 means *to succeed, to finish, to complete* and has the spear, the halberd as its radical. Finally, 果 refers to *fruit* and *result*, with an ideographic of a fruit growing on a tree.

5 MAKING INTERCULTURALITY WORK TOGETHER... 117

This discourse instrument urges us to consider how the achievements of others (here: outsiders, 'foreign cultures') can contribute to our own societies, cultures, well-being, development by absorbing their ideas, productions, artefacts. In the second chapter, we discussed extensively the concept of culture and how it indicated change, mixing and mélange in the Chinese language. 吸收外国文化有益成果 has always contributed to enriching and transforming cultural habits, values and artefacts throughout the centuries in China and the rest of the world.

他山之石, 可以攻玉—*Tā shān zhī shí, kěyǐ gōng yù*
Can be translated as: *Stones from other mountains/hills can serve to polish jade.*

This instrument declines as follows: 他 (tā, with an ideographic of an additional person) for *he, other, another*; 山 (shān, pictographic: three mountain peaks) for *the mountain, hill* (and anything that resembles a mountain); 之 (zhī, ideographic: a foot, i.e. to follow) for *him, her, it*; 石 (shí, an ideographic for a rock at the base of a cliff) for *stone, stone inscription*; 可以 (kěyǐ) for *can, may, possible*; 攻 (gong) for *to attack, to accuse, to study*; and 玉 (yù, ideographic: a necklace adorned with three pieces of jade) for *jade*.

What this discourse instrument means is that people/foreigners can assist others or another country, providing advice or helping others find solutions for all kinds of problems that they might want to solve. Learning from/with others, using them for what they do better than us, while creating bonds, understanding and respect can boost interculturality long-term, if 'done' genuinely.

Learning Togetherness

多元一体教育—*Duō yuán yī tǐ jiào yù*
Can be translated as: *(word-for-word translation:) Multi-in-one education; multi-integrated, multicultural education; Minzu education.*

Three sets of characters compose this instrument: 多元 (duō yuan) for *poly-, multi-*; 一体 (yī tǐ) refers to *an integral whole, everybody*; 教育 (jiào yù) means *education*. 教 is the Chinese character for *religion, teaching, to tell* and is based on the sub-character for *script* which conveys its meaning.

The character is found in words such as *professor, teaching and learning, to instruct*. 育 defines as *to have children, to raise* or *bring up, to educate* and has an ideographic of a pregnant woman with a baby in her womb.

多元一体教育 is known as *unified pluralist education*. This type of education aims to support and educate people for diversity in unity, entitling them to learn about, for example, their own and other Minzu groups and languages (if they have a specific language) while at the same time focus on what Chinese people all have in common (such as Chinese culture as the contribution of all Minzu cultures), what they can achieve together and making sure that they can learn to use the Chinese language to allow inclusion, equality/equity and building up oneness and a sense of togetherness.

As a reminder, a comparison and an example, the French Constitution presents similar ideas when it states in Article 1 that "The French Republic is indivisible, secular, democratic and social", and in Article 2 that "The language of the Republic shall be French".

民族团结教育—*Mín zú tuán jié jiāo yù*
Can be translated as: *Education for Minzu unity.*

In this discourse instrument, 团结 (tuán jié) means *to unite, unity, united*, and *solidarity*. 团 translates as *round, ball, to gather* and has an ideographic of a lot of talent gathered in one place. 结 is based on the sub-characters of *silk/thread, lucky, propitious, good* and means *a knot, sturdy, bond.*

Minzu unity education aims to let students learn and reflect on knowledge about all the 56 Minzu groups (culture, history) but also about Minzu policies (e.g. Zhang & Chen, 2014). The ultimate goal is to empower students to communicate with members of different Minzu groups and to promote mutual exchanges—and thus interculturality.

双语教育—*Shuāng yǔ jiāo yù*
Can be translated as: *Bilingual education.*

双语 (Shuāng yǔ) means *bilingual* (the capacity to use two languages). 双 is *two, double, pair*, with an ideographic of two hands side-by-side. 语 is based on a sub-character for *words, speech*, which conveys its meaning. It means *dialect, language* and *speech*.

In English, bilingual comes from Latin *bilinguis* meaning literally *two-tongued*, and, figuratively, *speaking a jumble of languages*. *Bilinguis* was also used to refer to *double-tongued, hypocritical,* and *false*.

53 of the Minzu groups have their own languages. Improving Minzu education in China means improving the linguistic abilities of Minzu students in their own Minzu language(s) and in Mandarin Chinese. Some preferential policies have been formulated for preparing and training bilingual teachers and for developing teaching materials. It is important to note that, like most countries in the world, the study of the 'common language' (the Chinese language here) is compulsory for all students to ensure communication, integration and building up a sense of community.

增进共同性、尊重和包容差异性—*Zēng jìn gòng tóng xìng, zūn zhòng hé bāo róng chā yì xìng*

Can be translated as: *Promote commonality, respect and tolerance of differences.*

The discourse instrument is based on seven sets of characters: 增进 (zēng jìn) for *to promote, to advance*; 共同 (gòng tóng, ideographic for 共 is two hands holding one object and for 同 is sharing a common tongue) for *common, joint, together*; 性 (xìng) for *nature, quality, property*; 尊重 (zūn zhòng, 尊 means *to honour, respect* and has an ideographic of a hand making an offering of wine while 重 has an ideographic of a burden carried for a thousand miles) for *to esteem, to respect, to value*; 和 hé for *together with, union and harmony*; 包容 (bāo róng) for *to pardon, to forgive, to show tolerance* and 差异性 (chā yì xìng, 差 has an ideographic of work done by a sheep (i.e. incompetence); 异 an ideographic of a person with a scary face) for *difference*.

In English, the word *tolerance* comes from Latin *tolerare* for *to bear, endure, tolerate*. The word took on its meaning as free from bias or acute judgement of others at the end of the eighteenth century.

While promoting exchanges and unity of all Minzu groups, this discourse instrument recommends looking for and promoting similarities, and considering differences under the lens of tolerance and respect.

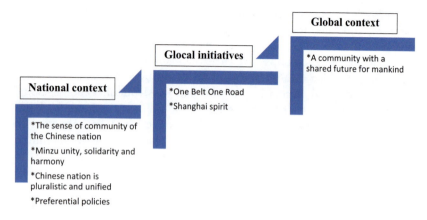

Fig. 5.4 Chinese initiatives for (glocal) interculturality

Pause

This chapter was dedicated to discourse instruments related to today's 'Chinese stories of interculturality' (with many links to past references). Different levels were identified from the national (e.g. Minzu policies) to the global (international governance).

Figure 5.4 summarizes the many and varies political initiatives that we have presented. Three contexts are proposed: national, glocal (local + global) and global.

Many of the discourse instruments have helped us unthink and rethink the links between interculturality and togetherness. Metaphors of *the sky, the sea, lips* and *teeth* but also parrallelisms whereby two entities are interrelated such as *you and me, common ground and differences*, are used in the instruments to indicate togetherness at micro- and/or macro-levels. Figure 5.5 displays these instruments.

Finally, the chapter introduced a certain number of educational initiatives related to glocal interculturality in Mainland China (see Dervin & Yuan, 2021; Sude et al., 2020), for example, 多元一体教育 (duō yuán yī tǐ jiào yù, *Multi-in-one education; multi-integrated, multicultural education; Minzu education*); 民族团结教育 (mín zú tuán jié jiāo yù, *education for Minzu unity*), 双语教育 (shuāng yǔ jiāo yù, *bilingual education*) (see Fig. 5.6). These are meant to promote inclusiveness, a sense of brotherhood and coming together. We recommend getting acquainted with these perspectives as a potential source of inspiration and reflexivity.

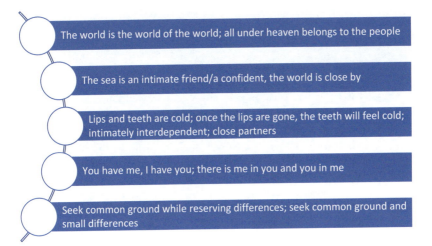

Fig. 5.5 Interculturality and togetherness

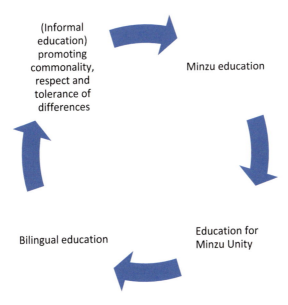

Fig. 5.6 Learning togetherness in the Chinese context

Thinking Further

- Which of these three words are often used in your own context: *togetherness, group(ness)* and *community*? Who uses them and for what purpose(s)? Do you use them yourself? What meaning(s) would you give to them?
- Go back to the etymology of the word for *community* in the languages that you know. Can you find some interesting 'archaeological' features behind the word? Discuss them in relation to interculturality.
- What metaphors are used in the discourse instruments contained in this chapter, to refer to and reflect togetherness (see the example of pomegranates)? What about in your context? What metaphors are used?
- Can you list discourse instruments put forward by decision-makers in your own context and at supra-national levels to urge people to reflect on and feel towards togetherness?
- After reading this chapter, what do you make of the notion of Minzu (民族)? Try to explain it in your own words.
- A few Minzu groups are mentioned in the chapter (e.g. *the Han, Hui, Mongolian, Uygur, Zhuang Minzu groups*). Try to find some information about these groups. Reflect on your findings, especially in relation to interculturality.
- Is the idea of 'national unity' central in education and politics in your context? How is it understood and how does it manifest in these spheres?
- Reflect on how tolerant politics and education are towards *difference* in your own context. What differences are easily included and excluded in schools for example? How much are they promoted, accepted and celebrated, and why?
- Review critically and reflexively the discourse instrument of *Absorbing the good sides of foreign cultures* (吸收外国文化有益成果).
- In many of the discourse instruments that we have seen hitherto, the ideas of *interconnection* and *reciprocity* are omnipresent and are very much in line with the idea of interculturality. How do you understand them in relation to interculturality and how do you view them for your future encounters?

(*continued*)

(continued)

- What are your views on preferential policies in general? Do you think that they promote equality/equity? Explain why.
- Have you heard of the One Belt One Road initiative? Can you recall what kinds of facts and opinions were shared about it and by whom? Can you speculate as to why they might have had these ideas?
- While you were reading the chapter, you probably noted recurring keywords and notions in the Chinese discourse instruments. Can you list them and try to explain what they mean?
- Some of the discourse instruments from this chapter hint at the need to learn from 'outsiders', 'foreigners' to improve oneself. Do you know similar instruments in your language(s)?
- How to reconcile diversity, similarity and unity in education? How is this 'done' in your country?
- Are issues for example, of well-being and economic development openly discussed in relation to interculturality in your context (e.g. in education)? If not, under which other keywords might they be found?
- Do some research on 大同 (Great Harmony)—a Confucian concept for an ideal society. Are there any new ideas related to it that you find inspiring for reflecting on togetherness and interculturality?
- Do you agree with the idea that coexistence facilitates interculturality?
- How do you understand the idea of close partnership in relation to interculturality? How can this work?
- What do you make of the values of *equality, self-respect, happiness, freedom, safety* and *development* put forward in relation to the discourse instrument of 民族情怀? Do you think that these are universally understood the same way in different societies around the world?
- What potential problems one might face combining unity and plurality in intercultural relations?

(*continued*)

> (continued)
> - Try to find out a bit more about the idea of 天下 (Tiānxià). Has it been discussed and problematized in your context and in the languages that you know? What general impression of how it is being paid attention to do you note?
> - How many of the official discourse instruments from the first section of this chapter have you ever heard of? Can you summarize what you have learnt about them and how they can make you think further about interculturality from a broader perspective?

References

Bauman, Z. (2000). *Liquid Modernity*. Polity Press.

Constitution of the People's Republic of China. (1982). http://www.npc.gov.cn/zgrdw/npc/zt/qt/gjxfz/2014-12/04/content_1888197.htm

Dervin, F., & Yuan, M. (2021). *Revitalizing Interculturality in Education. Chinese Minzu as a Companion*. Routledge.

Fei, X. (2015). *Globalization and Cultural Self-Awareness*. Springer.

Sude, Yuan, M., & Dervin, F. (2020). *An Introduction of Ethnic Minority Education in China: Policies and Practices*. Springer.

Sutherland, C. (2017). *Reimagining the Nation: Togetherness, Belonging and Mobility*. Polity Press.

Zhang, D., & Chen, L. (2014). Creating a Multicultural Curriculum in Han-Dominant Schools. *Comparative Education, 50*(4), 400–416.

Zhao, T. (2021). *All Under Heaven: The Tianxia System for a Possible World Order*. University of California Press.

CHAPTER 6

Learning to 'Do' Interculturality: *Setting Objectives for Oneself*

INTRODUCTION

Reflexivity has been both an implicit and explicit *modus operandi* and an outcome of intercultural encounters in education and beyond over the past decades (Byrd Clark & Dervin, 2014; Freda et al., 2016). Although reflexivity was not systematically created, developed or applied, it occurs in some way or another when we engage with other people. As such, through gazing at them, co-creating words, sentences and discourses (but also actions), willy nilly, we start listening to ourselves, observing what we do and look like, and react (or not) accordingly. By evaluating situations of encounters, we make decisions about what we do and say, with the other.

Chinese stories of interculturality from the past and today do emphasize reflexivity and criticality. The enmeshment of self-other has always been discussed in these stories and thus the influence we have on others and vice-versa—for better or worse. In this section, we review discourse instruments that urge and help us 'do' interculturality by looking inside ourselves and, at the same time, observing, how self and other influence each other. Input from Chinese thinkers and philosophers such as Confucius (孔子, 551–479 BCE) and Mencius (孟子, 371–289 BCE) will be made use of in what follows (see Fig. 6.1).

© The Author(s), under exclusive license to Springer Nature Switzerland AG 2022
M. Yuan et al., *Change and Exchange in Global Education*, Palgrave Studies on Chinese Education in a Global Perspective, https://doi.org/10.1007/978-3-031-12770-0_6

Fig. 6.1 References to Mencius, Xunzi and the Analects by Confucius on a street panel. The big characters on both sides of the panel are 礼 (Li, i.e. ritual) and 智 (Zhi, wisdom, knowledge)

This chapter contains four sections: Looking at the Self, Reflecting on 'Doing' Interculturality with the Other, Practicing Complexity and Plurality and Modesty in Reflexivity.

Looking at the Self

The mirror represents an important metaphor to symbolize reflexivity. Looking at self while scrutinizing the other, as if the other was an echo, reflecting on what we see in this mirror, can help us communicate with each other: we can observe what we do, how we speak, how these seem to impact the other, while examining and acting upon how the way they speak and act for/with us shapes and changes us.

君子—Jūn zǐ
Can be translated as: *Man of virtue; person of noble character; nobleman.*

君 (jūn) means *the monarch, lord, gentleman* and *ruler*. Its ideographic is that of a leader giving orders. 子 (zǐ) can have multiple meanings in English: *son, child, seed, small thing* and it is also an ancient Chinese compass point (0°, north). Its ideographic represents a child in a wrap, with outstretched arms but bundled legs.

One of the English translations of this discourse instrument is *gentleman*, from the adjective *gentle*. Latin *gentilis* for *of the same family* or *clan* provides its etymology, with the keywords of *race, clan*, and to *give birth* as roots. *Noble* comes from Latin *nobilis* for *well-known, famous, renowned* and *of superior birth*.

君子 is an important Confucian figure, a man of virtue who pursues and practises the ideal known as *The Tao* (名词), signifying the Way, a specific code of behaviour, when one is in harmony with the natural order. In Confucius's times, society was chaotic, corrupt and unjust, thus the figure of the 君子 was put forward as an example of what a good person should be, especially in relation to others. This discourse instrument carries a moral meaning: 君子 must do things right and follow etiquettes if they are deemed ethically appropriate. It refers to an erudite who asks questions carefully, reflects on what and how to do something right. What is more, the Jūnzǐ does not speculate. 君子 is also someone who has respect for others and who is a faithful, benevolent and righteous person. Self-cultivation, for which reflexivity, that is, looking at oneself critically, is at the centre of this discourse instrument.

Interculturality requires both moral and intellectual engagement with our position in the world. Unthinking what we think is *right, wrong, beautiful, ugly, interesting, dull, ethical, unacceptable,* and so on, while engaging with others, and rethinking these aspects with them correspond to two very important aspects of interculturality. We should not jump to conclusions, speculate about who people are and why they do things in certain ways. Opening to and with the other is engaging seriously in discussions around these issues, while looking inwards and accepting that we must see ourselves (what we think, accept and condemn) from multiple angles. These are painful processes since we are not always ready to accept 'defeat', being 'wrong' and changing our mind, opinion, actions but they are necessary to accept change. Finally, one element that we can learn from 君子 is the importance of asking questions—'real' questions leading to looking at oneself from the outside—to others so that we can move forward together, being 'transformed' together (*inter*-culturality). Ethics, as an important component of interculturality, must be systematically taken into account in, for example education. Making people reflect on why and how they do and say things with others matters more than 'forcing' them to speak and behave in certain preferred ways. Ethics does not necessarily provide right or wrong answers but it urges us to take the time to think about self, other, the surroundings, the world—and not to rush into doing things right *only*. By unthinking, rethinking and dialoguing around what we do and say with others, observing our potential mistakes, rectifying our actions, words and behaviours (again and again), we can move forward in a form of interculturality that is processual, fairer and transformative.

仁者爱人—*Rén zhě ài rén*

Can be translated as: *A benevolent person loves others; the benevolent person has a loving heart.*

Four characters compose this discourse instrument:

- 仁 (rén, ideographic: a caring relationship between two people) for *humane* and *kernel*. It is based on characters for *people + two* and is found in Chinese phrases for *to treat everyone equally favourably* and *not to discriminate*;
- 者 (zhě) for *person involved in*. It is based on characters for *old, aged* and *experienced* as well as *sun, day*;
- 爱 (ài) means *to love, to be fond of*. It has an ideographic of *to bring a friend into one's house*;
- 人 (rén) refers to *a person* and *people*, with a pictographic of the legs of a human being.

The English translation of the discourse instrument includes the adjective *benevolent*, which is not very commonly used in the language today. The word is based on Latin *bene* for *well* and *volentem* for *to wish*. Someone who is benevolent is sympathetic, considerate, and wishing others well.

Renzhe (仁者) refers to benevolent and virtuous people or people with loving hearts, who have tremendous courage, wisdom, charm, charisma and, most importantly, a perfect moral character. They love and care for others. Confucianism holds *rén* (仁) as the highest moral value (see Fig. 6.2). This could be considered as an important aspect of interculturality, especially in helping us reflect on how we behave with others, treat them and, most importantly, treasure their co-presence and sympathy.

Fig. 6.2 The character for 仁 (*rén*, benevolence) on a rock

Benevolence is an ideal and cannot always be achieved since it depends on the behaviours of others and the different contexts where we meet. However, it can inspire us to reflect on what we do with others and to think of strategies to do 'better'.

反求诸己—*Fǎn qiú zhū jǐ*
Can be translated as: *Turn inward and examine yourself when you encounter difficulties in life; to seek the cause in oneself rather than in somebody else; to think behind closed curtains; moral cultivation.*

The idea of this discourse instrument is found in many other Chinese discourse instruments such as: 上等人反求诸己 次等人责怪他人 (superior people blame themselves; the inferior blame others); 当我们见到人们乖张的个性 我们应内省反求诸 (When we see men of a contrary character, we should turn inwards and examine ourselves).

The instrument is based on: 反 (fǎn) for *contrary, to reverse, opposite* and *against*, with an ideographic of a hand held up against a cliff; 求 (qiú) for *to seek, to request, to demand*; 诸 (zhū) for *all, various* (with the sub-character for words, speech conveying its meaning) and 己 (jǐ) for *self, oneself*, whose pictographic is a loom woven with thread.

This discourse instrument, urging for moral cultivation of self, is from Mencius. Reflecting on one's own faults and correcting them without blaming others are at the centre of this instrument. It requires us to think 'behind closed curtains', to reflect on what we think and do (e.g. with the other) and to find alternative ways of thinking and doing if necessary. To turn inward can also prevent us from too easily accusing/blaming the other and disparaging them. When we speak and do things with other people, we both take, somehow, responsibility for the end result since we co-construct words, actions, attitudes. Instead of jumping to conclusions as to why something has happened to us, there is a need to examine ourselves first and then to look at the broader picture—again, *with* the other. Ideally, reciprocity in turning inwards would enrich interculturality.

怨天尤人—*Yuàn tiān yóu rén*
Can be translated as: *To complain against heaven and bear a grudge against men; to blame the gods and accuse others.*

怨 (yuàn) translates as *to blame, to complain* and is based on a sub-character for *heart*; 天 (tiān) is *the day, sky* and *heaven* (ideographic: the heavens above a man; the character is found in words like *today, tomorrow, the weather*); 尤 (yóu) refers to *outstanding*, and is used sometimes to express discontentment against someone or something (a character for a person with damaged feet conveys its meaning); 人 (rén) is *a person, people*.

Found in *The Analects* this discourse instrument urges us to not complain uselessly or blame others when we face problems. Like the previous discourse instrument, it suggests that being self-aware, broad-minded and encouraging is critical when one deals with interculturality. Incriminating others (see scapegoating them), complaining about them and about our own problems, criticizing words and actions—although these are frequent thoughts and behaviours that we all 'do'—can be counterproductive in intercultural encounters.

The antonymic discourse instrument, 任劳任怨、自怨自艾 (Rènláorèn yuàn, zìyuànzìyì), means *to work hard and blame oneself.*

三省吾身—*Sān xǐng wú shēn*
Can be translated as: *Reflect on oneself several times a day; introspection.*

三 (sān, ideographic: three parallel lines) for *three*, found in, for example, the word for *triangle*; 省 (xǐng, with a sub-character conveying its meaning based on the words for *eye, to look at* and *division*) for *to save, to omit, to leave out*; 吾 (wú) for *I* and *my*; 身 (shēn, pictographic of a pregnant woman) for *body, life, the main part of a structure or a body*.

The English word *introspection*, which we have already introduced a few times, is based on Latin for *to look into, examine* and *observe attentively* (*introspicere, intro = inward* and *specere = to look at*). The meaning of action of searching one's feelings or thoughts dates back to the early nineteenth century.

This discourse instrument suggests to reflect often on what we do and say in order to self-cultivate and to do it from multiple angles (see the reference to number three in the instrument). Introspection can easily happen through the use of 'tools' such as diaries, confessions to friends and family, art, listening to music (see Foucault's, 1988 *Technologies of the Self*). Again, in intercultural situations, the focus on self, while 'doing' them with others, is central to move forward in the changes that interculturality presses us to experience. Without introspection and by just merely transposing what we wish for and from the other, the *inter-* of interculturality disappears.

知常达变—*Zhī cháng dá biàn*
Can be translated as: *(word-for-word:) Know how to change; be aware of change; master both permanence and change.*

知 (zhī) means *to know, to be aware*. The character for *the mouth* conveys its meaning; 达 (dá) is *to attain, to reach, to communicate* and has *walking* as a sub-character conveying its meaning. 变 (biàn) translates as *to change, to transform, to vary* and is based on two sub-characters, one for *also, too, likewise* and another one for *and, also*.

In English, the keyword of *change* is from Latin *cambire* for *to exchange, barter* and has its root in the ideas of bending and crooking.

The discourse instrument under review tells us that one should not only have a good command of the basic rules for acting, behaving and decision-making, but also of how to deal with exceptional situations or setbacks in a flexible way. The main idea is to learn how to stick to principles while adapting to circumstances—and thus change—whenever it is deemed necessary. The dialectic principles of permanence-change, standard-flexibility, solidity-liquidity (in reference to Z. Bauman's work, 2000) as well as universality-particularity need to be borne in mind when 'doing' interculturality. Balancing our responses to others based on such continua, while engaging in discussions with them about these principles, represents a priority of interculturality as change.

修己安人—*Xiū jǐ ān rén*

Can be translated as: *Cultivate oneself to benefit others; self-cultivation; self-betterment.*

Four characters compose this discourse instrument: 修 (xiū) can refer to *dried meat, to decorate, to build* and *to cultivate*. The sub-character for *hair* conveys the meaning of 修. 己 (jǐ) translates as *self, oneself* and has a pictographic of a loom woven with thread. 安 (ān) is polysemic and can mean *calm, secure, to fix, to pacify*. Its ideographic is that of a woman safe in a house. The character is found in words for *security, law and order* in Chinese.

The character 修 can translate as *to cultivate* in English, a word not often used in the language today, especially in a figurative way. *Cultivate* is based on Latin for *care, labour* and *cultivation*.

修己安人 refers to the constant improving and taking care of one's advancement, especially in terms of abilities and morality, in order to make contributions to society and other people. This instrument is from Confucius. The altruistic view of self-cultivation appears to be of interest for interculturality here and provides us with further motivation for getting better at 'doing' interculturality, beyond mere self-centeredness. When I get better in terms of abilities and morality, I am readier to meet and be with others, and to contribute to our relations, actions and shared humanity. It is important to note that self-betterment depends on the other too—their in/direct contributions being essential to 修己安人.

Reflecting on 'Doing' Interculturality with the Other

Both *the reasons and motivations for* and *ways of* 'doing' interculturality with the other should be part of our introspective routines: *why did I wish to interact with this person (was it my choice)? What did I get from our interaction? What worked well from my own perspective? What did not and why? What did I contribute to our exchanges? What change(s) did I (not) experience? What about the other?*

爱人为大—*Ài rén wéi dà*

Can be translated as: *Love people; being caring for people; caring for Others is the priority.*

为 (wéi) is polysemic and can mean *to serve as, to behave as, to be* or *to do*. It is based on the combination of the sub-characters for *strength, power, influence*. 大 (dà, ideographic: a man with outstretched arms) means *big, huge, great, wide*.

This discourse instrument is from Mencius. Being friendly and treating people well should be our main concern when interacting with others. The way we care about others often leads to other people caring for us. Since the ideas of love and caring for are polysemic, it is always important to be aware of similarities and differences in the ways they are understood, used (or not) and acted upon. This can help us avoid generalizing and imposing our views and actions on the other; we should never assume that they are shared universally. At the same time, by being vocal about our perceptions and understanding of love and care, we may create an atmosphere and relations in which people might feel more comfortable, and prevent them from feeling overwhelmed or confused. Since love and care relate to inner feelings, people may not express their discontentment or surprise. This is why when reflecting on 爱人为大 one should always try to see it from others' perspectives and to try to find ways to explore others' ('real') feelings.

礼—*Lǐ*

Can be translated as: *Rites, norms, manners, respectful attitude, ceremony* or *Li*.

礼 translates as *gift, rite, ceremony* but also *propriety, etiquette* and/or *courtesy*. It is based on a sub-character for *spirit*, which conveys its meaning and is found in words such as *wedding ceremony*.

Li (礼) is a discourse instrument referring to social norms (i.e. a code of conduct), which regulate an individual's relationship with other people, putting into action such values as tolerance, self-confidence and dignified appearance. Li has to do with the discourse instrument of benevolence. Originally, it referred to activities such as playing music, providing beautiful jade and wine as well as worshipping ancestors or gods. The idea of rituals is central to Li. As such, in order to make relations 'transparent', rituals remind people of what is expected/to expect from a specific situation and encounter in a given context. However, we need to bear in mind that rituals are not static and solid elements but that they can change and they can be modified together with others as we get to know each other better. As a starting point, rituals (e.g. politeness, ways of using certain words, daily routines) can also lead to interesting discussions around why we do things in certain ways, who decides what they entail and how they change. Renegotiating them so that everyone finds their own space and feels included should be systematically considered in interculturality.

换位 思考—*Huàn wèi sī kǎo*

Can be translated as: *To put yourself in the other person's shoes; mutual empathy and understanding; perspective taking.*

换 (huàn) translates as *to exchange, to change, to switch*, with the sub-character of the hand conveying its meaning. 位 (wèi) refers to *position, location, seat* and has an ideographic for the place where a person stands. The two characters 思考 (sī kǎo) placed together mean *to reflect on* and *to ponder over*. 思 (sī) is *to think* or *to consider* and has an ideographic of weighing something with one's mind. 考 (kǎo) means *to check, to verify, to examine* and has the sub-character for *old, aged* and *experienced* conveying its meaning.

This discourse instrument relates to the idea of empathy in English. The English word was modelled on the German *Einfühlung* ('in-feeling'), which is somewhat of a translation of Greek *empatheia* for *passion, state of emotion*.

换位 思考 urges us to try to put ourselves in other people's position when engaging with them so that we may see the world—*our worlds*—through different eyes and understand why people behave, think and speak differently in specific situations. At the same, mutual empathy and understanding can help us grasp our joint influence on what we do and say. By doing so, one can learn to try to think differently, to see things from different perspectives, to learn to trust others and to… change. By learning to observe and listen carefully to others (and others together with us), we may be able to give interculturality a chance of pushing us in new and diverse directions.

推己及人—*Tuī jǐ jí rén*
Can be translated as: *Self-cultivation; putting oneself in another's place.*

This discourse instrument shares similarities with the previous one.

推 (tuī) translates as *to push, to cut, to decline*, with the sub-character for *hand* conveying its meaning. 己 (jǐ) is *self, oneself*. 及 (jí) refers to *and, up to* and *in time for* and 人 (rén) is the character for *a person/people*.

This instrument reminds us to show consideration for others by attempting to put ourselves in their place, and sympathizing with them by 'walking in their shoes'. It is found in both Confucius and Mencius. We should bear in mind that it is not always possible to see the world entirely through the eyes of the other. It is thus better to try to imagine *in different ways* how they might feel about someone/something, why they might act in certain ways and how they might feel about what we are 'doing' together interculturally.

恕—*Shù*
Can be translated as: *Being considerate; to show forgiveness.*

恕 means *to forgive* and has *the heart* as a sub-character, conveying the meaning. It is found in idioms such as *excuse me for not keeping you company* or *no merit can wipe out one's faults*.

The idea of *forgiveness* in English comes from Old English *forgiefan* (*completely* + *to give*) for *to give, grant, allow* but also, for example, *to remit a debt, pardon an offence*.

This instrument is also about empathy and it urges us to reflect on what we would do in a situation as experienced by another person, and to offer forgiveness as a potential outcome. In intercultural situations, before judging someone for doing something we consider wrong, 恕 urges us to unthink and rethink perspectives, actions and words before acting.

水至清则无鱼, 人至察则无徒—*Shuǐ zhì qīng zé wú yú, rén zhì chá zé wú tú*
Can be translated as: *There is no fish when the water is too clear; one should not set the bar too high for a person.*

水 (shuǐ) means *water, river, beverage*, with an ideographic of a river running between two banks; 至 (zhì) is *to arrive, most, until*, with an ideographic of a bird alighting on the ground; 清 (qīng) translates as *clear, quiet, pure* and *clean*, with the sub-character of water conveying its meaning; 则 (zé) is *but, principle, to imitate, to follow* and has an ideographic of laws inscribed on a slate; 无 (wú) is for *not to have, no, to lack*, and contains the radical for *weak* and *lame*; 鱼 (yú) is *a fish* in Chinese and has a pictographic of a fish swimming upwards; 察 (chá) translates as *to inquire, to observe*, with *a roof* as a sub-character conveying its meaning; 徒 (tú) is *the disciple, the believer, on foot*, with the ideographic of walking in someone's footsteps.

This instrument, which goes hand in hand with introspection and tolerance, urges us not to criticize a person for failing to be perfect, thus asking us not to be too demanding with other people. In other words, 水至清则无鱼, 人至察则无徒 is about being inclusive and tolerant, and to reflect on what we do and think with and for others. Interculturality often occurs through comparing self and other, which can lead to feelings of superiority/inferiority, confidence/lack of confidence, trust/lack of trust and influence the way we treat and consider each other. Modesty and empathy can support us in dealing with these complex issues and making us feel that we are equal.

己所不欲, 勿施于人—*Jǐ suǒ bù yù, wù shī yú rén*
Can be translated as: *Do not do unto others, do not impose on others.*

己 (jǐ, pictographic of a loom woven with thread) translates as *self, oneself*; 所 (suǒ, ideographic: an axe swung at a door) can mean *actually, place*, and be used as a classifier for small buildings; 不 (bù) refers to *no, not*; 欲 (yù, with the sub-character for *to lack, to owe, to breathe* conveying its meaning) is *desire, appetite, lust*; 勿 (wù) translates as *do not*; 施 (shī, composed of the sub-characters for *square, rectangle* and the character for *an ancient tribe in South China*) is *to grant, to give, to carry out*; 于 (yú, composed of the sub-characters for *two* and *hook*) corresponds to *to go, to take, in, at,* and *by*.

This discourse instrument refers to what is commonly known as *The Golden Rule*, which has been formulated in different and similar ways around the world. The 'Western' version is known as "Do unto others as you would have them do unto you", which highlights proactivity (the Silver Rule "do nothing to others you would not have done to you" is more about restraint). The rule has both ethical and psychological characteristics, hinting at equality, fairness, generosity and potential reciprocity. Confucius introduced the notion in China. Although the Chinese version is formulated in a negative way ("do not do"), it is very much inspiring for reflecting on interculturality. Through engaging actively, reflexively and critically with the other around what we do and say, we can learn how to apply both the silver and golden rules.

不置褒贬—*Bù zhì bāo biǎn*
Can be translated as: *Passing no judgement on; neither praising nor criticizing.*

The discourse instrument is divided up into three sets of characters: 不 (bù) for *not, no*; 置 (zhì; with a sub-character for *net, network* conveying the meaning) for *to install, to place, to put*; 褒贬 (bāo biǎn) for *to appraise, to pass judgement on* but also *to speak ill of*. 贬 has an ideographic of devaluing currency.

Derived from the *Romance of the Three Kingdoms*, written over 600 year ago about the second and third century of the Han Dynasty, this discourse instrument refers to the need to refrain from praising or criticizing. Moderation, modesty as well as listening carefully to what others have to say can support understanding and sympathizing with them. These elements are also at the centre of this important aspect of interculturality.

Practising Complexity and Plurality

转益多师—*Zhuǎn yì duō shī*
Can be translated as: *Learn from many masters, form your own style.*

转 (zhuǎn, the sub-character for *a cart* conveys the meaning) means *to revolve, to turn, to walk about*; 益 (yì, ideographic of a container overflowing with water) is *benefit, advantage*; 多 (duō, ideographic: two nights— i.e. many) can translate as *many, much, multi-* and 师 (shī, ideographic: to skilfully wield a knife) is *the teacher, master, expert, model.*

This discourse instrument urges us to learn from people and objects as much as we can. We can all learn from each other and should thus look for change by observing, listening to, exchanging and interacting with others interculturally. The curiosity to do so, especially if genuine, could contribute to interculturality being taken more seriously. It is only through exchanges with and influences of many different sources that we can build up complex, multiperspectival and stimulating forms of change.

众盲摸象—*Zhòng máng mō xiàng*

Can be translated as: *(word-for-word translation:) Blindly touch the elephant; multitude of blind people touch an elephant; unable to see the big picture; to mistake the part for the whole.*

众 (zhòng) is the equivalent of *many, numerous* and *crowd* in Chinese, with an ideographic of three people representing a crowd; 盲 (máng) translates as *blind* and has an ideographic of losing one's sight; 摸 (mō) means *to feel with the hand, to touch, to stroke*—the character for *hand* conveying its meaning; and 象 (xiàng) is *an elephant*, based on a sub-character for a *pig/boar* and another one for *mouth*.

In a Buddhist story, blind men try to use touch alone to make sense of what an elephant is. Each man touches a different part of the animal and makes their own evaluation of what the elephant is: the tusk (*the elephant is a turnip*), the ear (*the elephant is a dustpan*), the tail (*the elephant is a snake*). After reporting their observations to each other, the blind men were unable to agree on what the giant animal is—failing to get a sense of the whole picture together. This discourse instrument can help us to think about interculturality in multiple ways. For example, one of the main problems of interculturality today is that, conceptually and scientifically, its complexity is compartmentalized around the world with one or two paradigms winning over others (e.g. 'critical interculturality' *à la* 'Western' and 'culturalism' whereby culture is used to explain everything that people do and say, see Dervin & Yuan, 2021; Dervin & Jacobsson, 2022; Croucher, 2017; Halualani, 2017). Interculturality thus appears to be denied the right to be *really complex*, scholars and educators just 'feeling' one part of the body of the elephant. When one is aware of this simplification of interculturality, one can start building a more complex picture by joining different parts of the puzzle. Curiosity to do so also counts as an important aspect of questioning 众盲摸象.

齐物—*Qí wù*

Can be translated as: *Seeing things as equal; reconciling differences and contradictions among things.*

The two characters for 齐物 (qí wù) mean:

- 齐 (qí): *neat, level with, simultaneous, identical.*
- 物 (wù): *a thing, object, matter*—based on the sub-character for *ox* to convey its meaning.

This discourse instrument is from Zhuangzi and reminds us that everything is always the result of a mélange of opposites. Considering differing ideas and contradictions can help us open to complexities and alternative realities, and avoid thinking that only *we* hold some kind of 'truth'. Discussions around interculturality as both a phenomenon ('intercultural encounters') and a scientific and educational object deserve to be based on the principle of this instrument. In this book, we show that, for example, the use of words, concepts and notions in the English language globally, should include systematic discussions of their meanings and connotations in order to ensure equal, transparent and critical insights.

鉴古知今—*Jiàn gǔ zhī jīn*

Can be translated as: *Learn from the past and study the present; review the past to understand the present.*

鉴 (jiàn, with a radical referring to *metal*) translates as *example, mirror, to view* (character found in words such as *to learn from, to appraise* in Chinese); 古 (gǔ, ideographic: words passing through ten mouths) means *ancient, old*; 知 (zhī, with the sub-character *mouth* conveying its meaning) is *to know* and *to be aware* in English; 今 (jīn, ideographic: a mouth talking about things) is the equivalent *to current, contemporary* in English.

This instrument suggests considering the past and history to understand, problematize and reflect on strategies for today and the future, thus hinting at the interrelations between past, present and future. The first character depicts *a mirror*—history as a mirror for the present and the future. Although we are often made to believe that interculturality is a 'twenty-first century issue', it is clear that through engagement with philosophy, fiction, art, from the past, we can enrich and enlarge the way we see it today. As such, we are often surprised at how 'contemporary' some ideas from the past can be but also how, by 'digging' into it, we can understand how and why we 'do' interculturality in certain ways today.

读万卷书, 行万里路—*Dú wàn juàn shū, xíng wàn lǐ lù*

Can be translated as: *Read more walk more; read ten thousand books and travel ten thousand Li*, but also: *Learn as much as you can and do all you can.*

读 (dú, ideographic: to show off one's literacy) means *to read, to study*; 万 (wàn) is equivalent to *ten thousand* (i.e. *a great number*); 卷 (juàn, ideographic: a curled up scroll) translates as *to roll up, to carry on* (found in words like *a cigarette, a film*); 书 (shū, ideographic: a mark made by a pen) is *a book, a letter, a document*; 行 (xíng, ideographic: to take small steps with one's feet), translates as *to walk, to travel, temporary*; 里 (lǐ, ideographic: a unit of measure for farm land) mean *a li* (ancient measure of length = 500 m); 路 (lù) is *a journey, route*.

This discourse instrument urges people to read and to learn from other people's experiences. It stresses the importance of being curious about others and about learning in general and promotes travelling to go see for ourselves, as a complement to reading. 读万卷书, 行万里路 is also used to refer to *people who read a lot and travel a lot*. The idiom *travel broadens the mind* might partially overlap with this discourse instrument. We note however that travel does not necessarily open up our mind, especially if *we are not prepared to unprepare to do so* (Dervin & Jacobsson, 2021). Seeing different places, meeting diverse people, tasting different kinds of foods, do not automatically lead to interculturality as change, if one does not work and learn from others—hence, for example, the importance of reading to start thinking otherwise.

君子不器—*Jūn zǐ bù qì*

Can be translated as: *A gentleman is not an implement/a vessel.*

器 (qì) is *a device, a tool, a utensil* or *a vessel*. The character has the ideographic of four cooking vessels guarded by a dog. It is used in Chinese words for *weapons, machines* and *instruments*.

This discourse instrument is from Confucius. It suggests examining the bigger picture, and not remaining stranded in limited views and knowledge (see the metaphor of *the vessel* in the instrument). Opening up one's mind in the way we think about different aspects of life, self and other and the world is central to a form of interculturality that leads to change and exchange. This requires modesty, reflexivity and intellectual curiosity. Being satisfied with one's knowledge and unwilling to learn more or question ourselves are signs of being an 'implement/vessel'.

日新月异—*Rì xīn yuè yì*

Can be translated as: *Constant renewal; every day sees new developments; rapid progress.*

日 (rì) is *sun, day, date* (and *Japan*) in Chinese, it has a pictographic for the sun; 新 (xīn, ideographic: a freshly chopped tree) means *new* (found in the name of the Chinese Region called *Xinjiang*); 月 (yuè, pictographic of a crescent moon) means *moon, month*; 异 (yì, ideographic of a person with a scary face) translates as *different, other, unusual, to discriminate*.

This instrument, like the previous one, urges us to move forward in our learning and thinking and to open up constantly to both new ideas and new opportunities for learning. Interculturality as change should be considered as a catalyst and an incentive for constant renewal.

MODESTY IN REFLEXIVITY

满招损, 谦受益—*Mǎn zhāo sǔn, qiān shòu yì*
Can be translated as: *Complacency leads to failure, modesty to success; conceit and complacency cause failure whereas modesty and prudence bring success.*

满 (mǎn, contains the sub-character for *water* which conveys the meaning) translates as *full, packed, to satisfy*; 招 (zhāo, ideographic: a call to arms) means *to recruit, to incur, a manoeuvre*; 损 (sǔn, the sub-character for *hand* conveys the meaning) is the equivalent to *to decrease, to damage*; 谦 (qiān, with a sub-character for *speech, to speak*, ideographic: something passed from one hand to another) is *modest* in Chinese; 受 (shòu, meaning *to receive, to accept*) and 益 (yì, meaning *to benefit, advantage, to add*, ideographic: a container overflowing with water) together translate as *to benefit from, to profit*.

The discourse instrument includes the English word *modesty* in its translation. The word comes from Latin *modestia* for *moderate, sober, gentle* and *temperate* (from *modus: measure, manner*). The current meaning of *modesty* is from the end of the sixteenth century.

What the instrument reminds us is that humility about for example, one's achievements or one's country should surpass complacency, since the former can bring more 'success'. Showing off about oneself implicitly or explicitly in front of another person might trigger feelings of injustice, envy or discrimination and must thus be replaced by modesty to allow encounters to take place as equals or as people who have both achieved, in their own ways. This instrument links up with the idea of confidence, which must be treated carefully, finding a middle ground between low and over-confidence. It appears impossible to meet the other if we are either overly confident or lacking confidence about what we represent and how we are perceived.

虚一而静—*Xū yī ér jìng*
Can be translated as: *Void and quiet, open-mindedness, concentration and tranquillity.*

虚 (xū, ideographic: a tiger stalking in the bushes) means *emptiness, void*; 一 (yī) is *one, whole, single*; 而 (ér) translates as *and, as well as*, and *so*; 静 (jìng, the sub-character for *nature, young* and *blue, green, black* conveys its meaning) is *still, calm, not moving.*

This instrument from one of the architects of Confucian thought, Xunzi (Warring States period), asserts that one can get a correct understanding of things/people by observing them with an open mind, concentration and tranquillity. Approaching things and people without self-reflection, multiple perspectives or tolerance leads to a kind of interculturality that could be narrow, uncooperative and problematic—showing the way to *a status quo*, an antonym to *change*.

慎思明辨—*Shèn sī míng biàn*
Can be translated as: *Think carefully and discern; careful reflection and clear discrimination.*

慎 (Shèn, the sub-character for heart conveys its meaning) translates as *careful* and *cautious*; 思 (sī, ideographic: weighing something with one's mind and heart) is *to think, to consider* (character included in words for *ideology, train of thought*); 明 (míng, ideographic: the light of the sun and moon) and 辨 (biàn, ideographic: to separate two alternatives) together mean *to discern, to distinguish clearly.*

The instrument suggests being curious and tolerant, and to learn new knowledge as much as possible and as often as one can. At the same time, one needs to think carefully about what one learns and reflect on how to practise new and diversified knowledge—which requires building up reflexivity and criticality to do so. Obtaining new knowledge from different parts of the world and contexts about different aspects of life, who we are as complex beings and our surroundings, cannot but enrich our worldviews and help us open up to others.

三思而行—*Sān sī ér xíng*

Can be translated as: *Taking action after having reflected several times; think thrice before acting; don't act before you've thought it through carefully.*

三 (sān) stands for *three* and is composed of three parallel lines; 思 (sī) translates as *to think, to consider*, with the ideographic of weighing something with one's mind and heart; 而 (ér) is *and, as well as, yet (not)*; 行 (xíng) has an ideographic of to take small steps with one's feet, it means *to walk, to travel, competent, behaviour*.

From *the Analects*, this discourse instrument is about reflecting, (re-)considering before doing and/or saying something. In interculturality, one might want to think 'thrice' in many conversations or situations of encounters, not to create too much tension or give a bad image of oneself and/or others. We might often misunderstand/non-understand what others say and do; this is why we need to be cautious not to act too quickly. It does not mean that we should censor ourselves or refrain from behaving/acting in certain ways but we should analyse the situation first, second and third, discuss with others and the one concerned and 'act', wishing to change and exchange with them.

实事求是—*Shí shì qiú shì*

Can be translated as: *Seek truth from facts; to be practical and realistic.*

实 (shí) translates as *matter, thing* and *work*; 事 (shì) refers to *matter, business, to work*; 求 (qiú) means *to seek, to look for* and *to demand*; and 是 (shì, ideographic: to speak directly) is *to be, is, are, am* in English.

This last instrument is omnipresent on most Chinese university campuses. 实事求是 urges us to identify true knowledge based on evidence, without any exaggeration or belittlement. An antonym in English could be 'fake news'. Interculturality requires behaving in a sensible, credible and honest way and to handle things according to the realities of a given

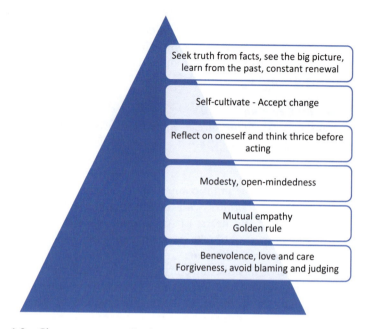

Fig. 6.3 Chapter summary (looking at oneself)

situation, refraining from voicing *but* revising one's biases, misrepresentations and stereotypes of self and other.

Discussion

This important chapter urges us to look inwards, to use the other as a mirror for observing ourselves. It asks us to reflect on ourselves and to think 'thrice' before talking and acting (see Fig. 6.3).

We started with the important Confucian figure of the 君子 (Jūnzǐ), a 'Man (sic) of virtue', a 'person of noble character' who shows benevolence, love and care for others. The Jūnzǐ also avoids judging and blaming, and is ready to show forgiveness.

Other discourse instruments—with some very similar to instruments used around the world—also call for mutual empathy, modesty and open-mindedness. Seeking truth from facts, seeing the big picture, learning from the past, and accepting and triggering constant renewal also represent rich learning resources for us. Finally, and most importantly, what all these instruments promote is that idea of self-cultivating and accepting change with the other.

When working with our students, we often ask them to reflect on the discourse instruments presented in this book. For a course on intercultural education, we proposed that they would look into a certain number of instruments related to reflexivity in learning to 'do' interculturality. We gave the following instructions to the students (they worked in both Chinese and English):

- Work in groups of three to five students; choose five Chinese discourse instruments for interculturality that could be used to give advice to people on how to do interculturality well.
- Determine how the five phrases can work together to create some model for 'doing' interculturality.
- Define each element in one sentence and make sure the definitions are very clear.
- Use your creativity to make a figure, a model, a table, and so on.

The students produced the following four posters in their respective groups, selecting some of the discourse instruments presented in this chapter, while explaining how they could fit together as a whole. What we notice is that many of the same instruments were selected by the students (e.g. *seek truth from facts*).

Group one (Fig. 6.4) decided to place the instruments in a pyramid, starting from *seeking truth from facts* as the 'basics' (their label/stage 1); moving on to *try to put yourself in their shoes* and *do unto others as you would have them to do unto you* (labelled as 'cultural difference'/stage 2); and finishing with *open-mindedness, concentration and tranquillity* and *investigate and check yourself* (reflect/stage 3). The full progression appears to be from culture-diversity to identity.

Group 2 (Fig. 6.5) focused on the Confucian figure of the Junzi as an ultimate goal for interculturality, and started from the foundational levels of *method* and *attitude*, moving towards *truth, reflection* and (deciding on)

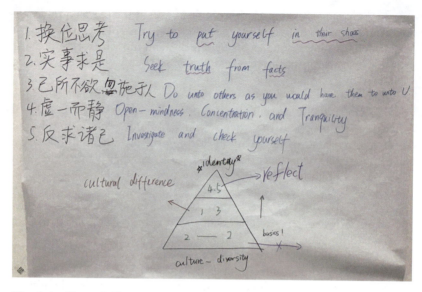

Fig. 6.4 Group 1: Try to put yourself in their shoes

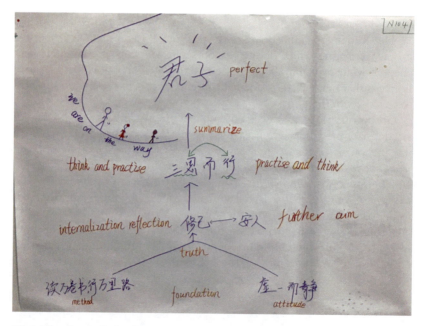

Fig. 6.5 Group 2: Perfect

6 LEARNING TO 'DO' INTERCULTURALITY: *SETTING OBJECTIVES...* 147

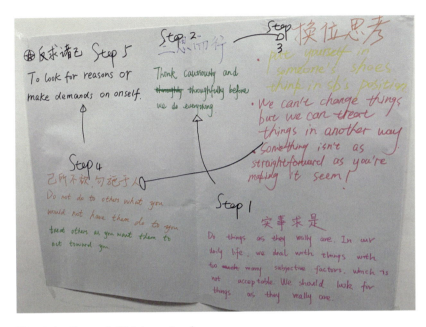

Fig. 6.6 Group 3: Think cautiously

further aim(s), leading to *think and practise* and *practise and think*, before summarizing.

Group 3 (Fig. 6.6) used a circle including five steps to demonstrate how some discourse instruments could be used to strengthen reflections on interculturality. The five steps are: Step 1—"Do things as they really are. In our daily life, we deal with things with too many subjective factors, which is not acceptable. We should look for things as they really are" (实事求是, *seek truth from facts*); Step 2—"Think cautiously and thoughtfully before we do everything" (三思而行, *taking action after having reflected several times, think thrice before acting*); Step 3—"Put yourself in someone's shoes. Think in somebody's position. We can't change things but we can treat things in another way. Something isn't as straightforward as

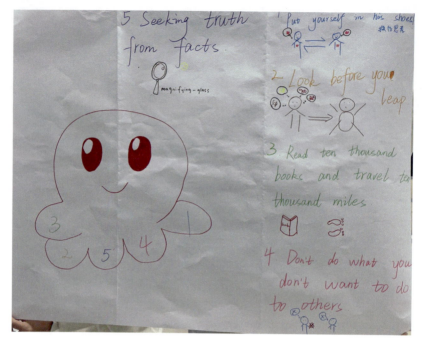

Fig. 6.7 Group 4: The octopus

you're making it seem!" (换位 思考, *mutual empathy and understanding*); Step 4—"Do not do to others what you would not have them do to you. Treat others as you want them to act toward you" (己所不欲, 勿施于人, *do not do unto others, do not impose on others*); Step 5—"To look for reasons or make demands on oneself" (反求诸己, *turn inward and examine yourself when you encounter difficulties in life*).

Group 4 (Fig. 6.7) uses the drawing of an octopus to present a model around the discourse instruments. These include: (1) Put yourself in his (sic) shoes; (2) Look before you leap; (3) Read ten thousand books and travel ten thousand miles; (4) Don't do what you don't want do to others (sic); (5) Seeking truth from facts.

Thinking Further

- The Confucian figure of the 君子 (*Jūnzǐ*) is known in English as *a Man of virtue; a person of noble character; a nobleman*. After reading the text about this discourse instrument, what word would you use in English to describe who they are, especially in relation to interculturality?
- Find out more about *The Tao* (名词). What aspects of this 'code of conduct' could be of interest for reflecting on interculturality?
- What do you make of the idea that "Ethics does not necessarily provide right or wrong answers but it urges us to take the time to think about self, other, the surroundings, the world—and not to rush into doing things right *only*"? Do you agree?
- Do you see love and care for others as priorities for interculturality? Is this how you usually treat strangers online and/or when and if you travel? Or do you somehow fear certain kinds of others? Why? Can you try to explain what/who might have influenced you in this regard?
- How could we make sure that there is reciprocity in 'turning inward and examining ourselves'? In other words, whenever we face a problem with an other, interculturally, how could we urge the other to examine themselves too in order for us to experience deep and transformative discussions?
- Explain this sentence in your own words: "Without introspection and by just merely transposing what we wish for and from the other, the *inter-* of interculturality disappears."
- Reflect on your own introspection. How do you do it on a daily basis? Do you use 'tools' such as diaries, blogs, chats with friends? How much does it influence your behaviours and ways of thinking?
- What comes to your mind when you hear the two keywords of *permanence* and *change*? Reflect on intercultural encounters that you have had (face-to-face and/or online) and try to identify how these two embedded elements of humanity and sociality have emerged from these encounters.

(*continued*)

(continued)

- Is the idea of *interculturality as change* becoming clearer at this stage? How would you define it in a few sentences?
- Following an interaction with someone, reflect on these questions: *Why did I wish to interact with this person? What did I get from our interaction? What worked well from my own perspective? What did not and why? What did I contribute to our exchanges? What change(s) did I (not) experience? What about the other?*
- Have you ever found yourself in an intercultural situation where signs and acts of love and care were too overwhelming (or confusing) for you? Were you able to renegotiate them with the other? How did you feel during the whole process?
- Can you think of rituals that you need to perform regularly? How did you learn them? Have you changed the way you 'do' them? Why and with whom? More specifically about interculturality: How can rituals be renegotiated so that as many people as possible can feel comfortable and included? Think of a concrete example.
- Are there people with whom you feel so comfortable and confident that you can 'walk in their shoes' and know how they 'really' feel? Who are they and why do you feel this way? Do you also think that there are people who can sympathize so much with you?
- In your interaction with people from other countries, how often do you feel that comparisons between cultures, languages and identities lead to someone feeling superior/inferior, confident/weak, and so on? What to do about this in order to rebalance power relations and to make sure that everyone is treated both implicitly and explicitly as equals?
- Which version of the Golden Rule are you aware of in different languages? What history/narrative of the discourse instrument do you know?
- Explain the discourse instrument 众盲摸象 (*multitude of blind people touch an elephant*) in your own words. What thoughts about interculturality as a phenomenon and as an object of research and education does it trigger in you?

(*continued*)

(continued)

- How often do you go back to the 'past' when you for example, examine, analyse and make decisions about how to treat others in interculturality? Can you give some concrete examples?
- Do you agree with our critique of the idiom "travel broadens the mind"? Weigh different opinions about our argument.
- Explain this discourse instrument in relation to interculturality: 君子不器—*A gentleman is not an implement/a vessel.*
- Do you sometimes find it difficult to balance different forms of confidence when you meet someone interculturally, between for example, *over-confidence* and *low confidence*? How to deal with these issues? And how to make sure that the other also reflects on them while interacting with us?
- Have you often found yourself in a situation where you acted without thinking carefully in intercultural contexts and had an unpleasant experience as a consequence? Had you misunderstood/non-understood what someone had said or done? How did you rectify the situation/action?
- How are/were you (being) prepared for 实事求是 (*Seek truth from facts; to be practical and realistic*) in formal and informal education? Do you feel that you know how to do this properly, especially when it comes to interculturality?

References

Bauman, Z. (2000). *Liquid Modernity*. Polity Press.
Byrd Clark, J., & Dervin, F. (2014). *Reflexivity in Language and Intercultural Education: Rethinking Multilingualism and Interculturality*. Routledge.
Croucher, S. (2017). *Global Perspectives on Intercultural Communication*. Routledge.
Dervin, F., & Jacobsson, A. (2021). *Teacher Education for Critical and Reflexive Interculturality*. Palgrave Macmillan.
Dervin, F., & Jacobsson, A. (2022). *Intercultural Communication Education. Broken Realities and Rebellious Dreams*. Springer.
Dervin, F., & Yuan, M. (2021). *Revitalizing Interculturality in Education. Chinese Minzu as a Companion*. Routledge.

Foucault, M. (1988). *Technologies of the Self.* University Massachusetts Press.
Freda, M. F., González-Monteagudo, J., & Esposito, G. (2016). *Working with Underachieving Students in Higher Education: Fostering Inclusion Through Narration and Reflexivity.* Routledge.
Halualani, R. T. (2017). *Intercultural Communication: A Critical Perspective.* Cognella Academic Publishing.

CHAPTER 7

Pondering over Language and Interculturality

Introduction

In this chapter, we focus on one aspect that is often neglected (surprisingly enough!) when one deals with interculturality: *language*. As it would have appeared clearly to our readers hitherto: there is no interculturality without language and no language without the *inter-* and *-ality* of interculturality. In other words, we cannot escape 'languaging' when we 'do' interculturality.

Language is understood here in broad terms (amongst others):

- *the materiality of language*: from the use of specific words to non-verbality in for example, using gestures to accompany one's co-constructed messages;
- *the aesthetics of language*: (subjective) evaluation and appreciation of sounds, written words, body postures and so on—that is, language as an evaluative and influential force;
- *language and identity*: how language triggers, reveals, constructs and categorizes who we (think we) are with and for others in simplified and/or complex ways—and vice versa;
- *language and sociality*: how we conduct, manoeuvre, see manipulate relations with others through language;

- *language and power*: how, through language, we are urged and forced to think in certain ways, to believe certain things about ourselves, others, the world, and so on.
- *the discursive layers in language use*: what we do with words with and for others—and vice versa;
- *the inside and outside of language*: how we see language as insiders and outsiders, within a given country/group of speakers and between different countries/speakers;
- *the indivisibility of language*: what I say—and do—is systematically imbedded in what others say and do/have said and done. Language is a constant flux, with no real beginning, no end;
- *silence and refusal to communicate*: these two aspects also represent important components of language.

More characteristics of language would deserve to be included here and we trust our readers will think of many others. The point that we wish to make is that *language does matter, language is always at the centre of everything* and it should be *systematically* taken into account in interculturality. This does not mean that one needs to be a linguist or 'gifted' for languages to do so—whatever this might mean. But we need to listen to, observe and be sensitive to the ways we use, perceive, review language together with others, the way it is used with us, how it affects us all and why.

China is, once again, a fascinating context to reflect on the multifacetedness of language use. Although outsiders often think about China as a monocultural and/or monolingual place, it will now have become obvious to our readers that it is not the case (Cheng, 2007). In what follows we wish to say some words about language in the Middle Kingdom as a way of introduction to this complexity.

First obvious but often ignored fact: Hundreds of dialects and languages are used in China on a daily basis.

The main language of China, the Chinese language, emerged within the Sinitic branch of the Sino-Tibetan languages, some 3000 years ago. It is represented today by a range of linguistic varieties spoken by most Chinese people. It is called 汉语 (Hànyǔ) and 中文 (Zhōngwén) to refer to it as a written language. Different spoken 'modes' of Chinese with different tones (up to 12 different ones) are used. Mandarin is the most spoken variety of Chinese, followed by the Min variety (e.g. Hokkien, Hainanese), the Wu (e.g. Shanghainese, Wenzhounese) and the Yue (e.g.

Cantonese spoken in the south of the country). As an example of the differences between these, we can mention the simple example of the number *one* which is pronounced *yī* in Mandarin, *it* in Hokkien and *yat* in Cantonese. Not all these varieties are necessarily interintelligible; however, most Chinese would consider them to be 'just' Chinese since they all share a same identity, history and culture. These varieties are often referred to as *fāngyán* (方言, literally *regional speech*) in Chinese while in English different (sometimes problematic) terms are used: *dialects, regionalects, topolects* and so on. The national language of China, adopted as a 'lingua franca' in the 1930s, is called Standard Chinese and derives from the Beijing dialect of Mandarin. Although, orally, Chinese speakers might use different forms of Chinese, and not necessarily understand when speaking to each other, they use the same written form, with slight differences between the simplified characters used in, for example Mainland China and Singapore, and the traditional characters in Hong Kong and Macau. Let's take the example of the word *strawberry* which is written 草莓 in both traditional and simplified Chinese but is pronounced *cǎo méi* in Mandarin and *sitó pélei* in Cantonese (influenced by English). It means that the way a given word is written in different Chinese varieties is more or less the same (traditional/simplified), while orally the pronunciation of the word might be completely different. If we try to make sense of this for English: Let's imagine that we see the word *telephone* in its written form and speakers of different 'dialects' of English pronounce it as (randomly) *carrot, apple* or *Tokyo*. Finally, let us remind our readers that Chinese also has Romanized written forms (use of Latin script), with *Hanyu Pinyin* as the most common (introduced in 1956). It also indicates the type of tones included in a word using accents on vowels (e.g. *cǎo méi*). In order to write a message on a phone a Chinese will use Pinyin to have access to Chinese characters.

About 300 other Minzu languages are spoken in Mainland China, divided up in at least 9 different groups: *Sino-Tibetan, Tai-Kadai* (spoken by e.g. the Dai and Zhuang), *Turkic* (e.g. Uyghurs), *Mongolic, Tungusic* (e.g. spoken by the Hezhe), *Korean, Hmong-Mien, Austroasiatic* (spoken by e.g. the Gin and Wa), *Austronesian* and *Indo-European* (spoken by the Russians and Tajiks) (see Figs. 7.1 and 7.2). In terms of writing, some languages have their specific written forms (e.g. the Kyrgyz, the Naxi) while others use Chinese characters such as the Zhuang.

This chapter is divided up into three sections: The Limits of Language/Misusing Language, Using Language in Interculturality and Qualifying

Fig. 7.1 An example of written Uyghur (From Minzu University of China Museum)

Language. This chapter is guided by Canetti's words about language (1989: 53): "When I read the words of this new (for me) language, my own words are filled with freshness and strength. The languages find their fountain of youth in one another."

Limits of Language/Misusing Language

In this first section we have collected discourse instruments that can help us reflect on what language *cannot do* or what we seem *unable to use language for*, and on aspects of language which can be detrimental when we misuse it *with* the other (and vice versa). Although this section might sound discouraging at first, it is meant to provide us with ways of rectifying these problems.

言不尽意—*Yán bù jìn yì*

Can be translated as: *Words cannot fully express thought; words don't exhaust ideas; to speak with reticence.*

Fig. 7.2 Northern Yi Dialect (From Minzu University of China Museum)

尽 (jìn) translates as *to use up, to end, finished, to the limit* and contains a sub-character for *a ruler, tape-measure, a unit of length*. 意 (yì) means *idea, meaning, wish, intention*, with the sub-character for *heart* conveying its meaning.

This discourse instrument is often found at the end of a letter in Chinese to tell one's correspondent that one is unable to express one's ideas fully. Identified in the *Book of Changes* this instrument reminds us that, although as humans we can use words to express ourselves, they are somewhat insufficient and will never allow us to describe and discuss the complexities of this world and of our life experiences and relations.

This is a good reminder for interculturality; at times, we may not feel that we can speak our mind or understand what the other is saying. Letting it go, accepting this reality and still trying to 'do' interculturality together one way or another is a lesson one can learn from this instrument. Time, cooperation and persistence might help us get closer to the meanings of things—or not. Our world is pushing for success in all aspects of 'communication', without reminding us that, on many occasions, we must accept that communication will fail and that we may not be able to make it happen 'properly'—whatever this might mean. One might want to reflect on this question at this stage: *is it better to miscommunicate/non-communicate* (the illusion that one communicates with others; pretending that we are communicating) or *to accept that one cannot construct and/or replicate the complexity of life and of the world in words, and use this last argument as a basis for meaningful conversations with others?*

言高语低—*Yán gāo yǔ dī*

Can be translated as: *High talk and low talk; to speak inconsequently and without discretion.*

Four characters compose this discourse instrument:

- 言 (yán) means *words, speech, to say* and *to talk*, with an ideographic of a tongue sticking out of a mouth. The character is used in words for *making a speech, a declaration* and *a spokesperson*.
- 高 (gāo) refers to *high, tall, loud* and has a pictographic of a tall palace. It is found in words for *happy, willing, to improve*, but also *university*.
- 语 (yǔ), a word we will come across repeatedly in this section, translates as *dialect, language* and *speech*. The character is built upon the sub-character for *words, speech* and *to speak*, which conveys its meaning.
- 低 (dī) is *low, beneath, to incline* and contains the sub-character for *man, person*.

This discourse instrument is used to refer to someone who has no sense of measure when they speak, navigating between *high talk* (e.g. formal/polite language) and *low talk* (e.g. using swearwords), without always noticing. This can produce discomfort and confusion in the other, and thus lead to refraining from interacting with them. Balancing language use is a means of creating a sense of hospitality, welcome, care and brotherhood interculturally, and a means of projecting an identity that the other will be willing to accept, co-construct and develop with the one speaking. This is why word choice in one's language and in another language is central to interculturality. At times we may not be aware that such or such word can be offensive to the other—or misinterpreted—hence the need to move away from 言高语低 or, at least, become aware of our own 'navigation' to learn to control it by observing the other's reactions.

前言不搭后语—*Qián yán bù dā hòu yǔ*
Can be translated as: *To utter words that do not hang together; can't connect back and forth; to talk/speak incoherently;* also: *self-contradictory*.

前 (qián) translates as *front, forward, top, before*, with an ideographic of feet on a boat with two poles (i.e. something is moving); 言 (yán) means *words, speech, to say* and *to talk*, with an ideographic of a tongue sticking out of a mouth; 不 (bù) plays the role of a negative prefix (*no, not*); 搭 (dā) can translate as *to build, to connect, to arrange in pairs*, with a sub-character for *the hand* conveying its meaning; 后 (hòu, ideographic: a person leaning forward to orders from a person's mouth) corresponds to *empress, queen, ruler* but also *behind, after* and *later*.

This instrument also hints at another potential problem in language use: when words seem isolated and disconnected, the thoughts that the utterer tries to express might appear confused and unjustified to the hearer/reader. Hence the need, in interculturality, to find ways of connecting 'back and forth' in what the other is saying, and to support others to do the same in relation to our own discourses. Instead of panicking when one faces 前言不搭后语, one needs to ask questions, listen carefully and support the other in their attempts to clarify their thoughts, *with and for* us (and vice versa).

修辞立诚—*Xiūcí lìchéng*
Can be translated as: *Rhetorical and honest; to establish credibility through careful choice of words; rhetoric is sincere.*

This instrument, which is the opposite of the previous one, is based on three sets of characters. (1) 修辞 (xiūcí, 修 = *dried meat, to embellish*, with the sub-character for *hair*; 辞 = *to resign, to decline*) means *rhetoric*; (2) 立 (lì) *to stand up, to establish, to draw up*, with a pictographic of a man standing on the ground; (3) 诚 (chéng): *sincere, authentic*, which contains the sub-character for *words, speech* and *to say*.

In English, the word *rhetoric* derives from Greek *rhētorikētekhnē* for *art of an orator* based on *rhētōr* for *a speaker, orator, artist of discourse* and *teacher of rhetoric*.

修辞立诚 is from the *Book of Changes*. Although this instrument referred originally to writing, what it hints at is important for any form of intercultural communication: speaking should reveal and thus correspond to the utterer's true intentions. Selecting carefully for example, words and sentences as well as discursive activities, is indispensable in *being with* the other if one wants to cultivate a relation and give meaning to it. Simplicity in expression can also support sincerity and integrity *for and with* the other. All in all, what the instrument urges us to do is to broaden the gap between discourse and action, as well as reality and lies. Trust in interculturality should start with 修辞立诚.

信言不美，美言不信—*Xìn yán bù měi, měi yán bù xìn*
Can be translated as: *Words are not beautiful, words are not believed; trustworthy words may not be fine-sounding; fine-sounding words may not be trustworthy.*

This discourse instrument is based on the use of four characters repeated twice in an opposite order:

- 信 (xìn) means *letter, to trust, confidence* (radical = character for *man* and *person*);
- 言 (yán) is for *words, speech, to talk*;
- 不 (bù) translates as a negative prefix;
- 美 (měi) corresponds to *beautiful, good, very satisfactory*, with an ideographic of a person wearing an elegant crown.

This discourse instrument comes from Laozi who suggested that writing should be unpretentious and spontaneous while avoiding using an excessive and frivolous style—and thus potentially misleading others and leading to exaggerations. When one learns to use a foreign language, one always has the impression (or is given the impression) that to speak the language properly, one needs to use 'sophisticated' and 'complex' language forms (sentences, words, etc.). This is however an illusion and, in fact, it can be detrimental to interactions with others. What matters is not the 'complicated' style but the will and stimulation to communicate with others. Straightforwardness and spontaneity represent two essential components of language use in interculturality. The instrument also applies to the attitudes we put into meeting others: flattering and deceiving others by using pleasing words will lead nowhere and create inequalities in relations. The performance that it leads to might be too overwhelming and making people uncomfortable and distrust speakers.

语焉不详—*Yŭ yān bù xiáng*
Can be translated as: *Speak and communicate superficially, not to speak in details.*

There are two characters of interest in this discourse instrument: 焉 (yān) for *where* and *how* (with an ideographic of a bird with a strange head) and 详 (xiáng) for *detailed* and *comprehensive*—the sub-character for *speech, words* conveying its meaning.

语焉不详 refers to discourses that are too brief or sketchy, not going into details. For interculturality, this can give an impression of for example, incompleteness, but also, depending on the context and interlocutor, hint at a lack of seriousness, see trigger the unacceptable stereotype of 'lower intellectual capacities'. Therefore, 语焉不详 should be collaboratively corrected if limiting the opportunities for being together meaningfully.

言多语失—*Yán duō yŭ shī*
Can be translated as: *He who talks too much is prone to make errors; if one says too much, one is bound to slip up at some point.*

Two new characters appear here: 多 (duō) stands for *many, much, more, multi-* (with an ideographic of two nights), (= many) and 失 (shī, ideographic: something falling from a hand) translates as *to lose, to fail*.

This instrument is about the link between quantity and quality of language, with the idea that if one uses too many words (many of which may not be relevant or useful), one wastes time and energy to think *with* the other, and can thus lead to making mistakes. Moderation in speaking matters in interculturality as was discussed earlier. Moderation from our own side means that we can give the floor to the other, listen to them, co-construct *with* them and thus trigger change in *both of us*.

夏虫不可以语冰—*Xià chóng bù kĕ yĭ yŭ bīng*
Can be translated as: *Summer bugs can't see/discuss ice; short-sighted without understanding the truth.*

夏 (xià) stands for *the summer*; 虫 (chóng) translates as *insects, worms* (amongst others); 可 (kě) is for *can, may, to permit, to suit*; 以 (yǐ) means *to use, by means of, because of*, with the radical of *a man, a person*; 冰 (bīng) refers to *ice, to chill something, cold* (ideographic: ice-cold water).

This discourse instrument revolves around the metaphor of a short-lived insect who will not experience the winter and thus be unaware of what ice is. The instrument urges us to open our mind to other realities and complexities. Interculturality requires from those who experience it to look beyond what they (think they) know and to be curious of other types of ideologies, experiences, feelings, meanings and actions, so that their own do not remain the only gauge for judging others. Pushing ourselves, challenging our views, ideas and sentiments, can make us see beyond the short-sightedness that often afflicts us in interculturality. Although we might be like 'summer insects', to refer back to the instrument, we must get used to seeing ice… and language is the most important tool that we can use to try to get a sense of what it is.

一语中人—*Yī yǔ zhōng rén*

Can be translated as: *Hurt people in one sentence; slander.*

一 (Yī) means *one, single* while 中 (zhōng, *middle*, ideographic: a line through the centre of a box) and 人 (rén, *man, person*) together refer to *a mediator, a go-between.*

This instrument refers to a situation whereby someone utters words that hurt the other. The English word, *slander*, summarizes well the gist of 一语中人: It is itself from Old French *esclandre* for *a scandalous statement* and thus shares its etymology with the word *scandal*. The English word as well as the discourse instrument might appear strong to some readers to describe intercultural situations where we tend to use stereotypes or biases when interacting with an other. However, although some of us might think that such discursive elements are 'harmless' and/or 'with a hint of truth about a people', those at the receiving end might feel hurt by such assertions. We need to beware of for example, stereotyping since it is a form of slander. The content of stereotypes usually informs us more of what the utterer thinks of themselves (as a positive opposite of the stereotype) and of their ideological positioning, identity construction and imaginaries (Ibelema, 2021; Abdallah-Pretceille, 2006; Ferri, 2018). It is thus worth reflecting on stereotypes from this perspective rather than trying to find some 'truth' about the other.

谗言佞语—Chán yán nìng yǔ
Can be translated as: *Words that slander others and flatter others.*

谗 (chán) means *to slander, to defame, to speak maliciously* and has a sub-character for *speech, to talk* conveying its meaning; 佞 (nìng) *to flatter, flattery*, with an ideographic of kindness towards a woman.

This instrument refers to situations where someone utters bad things about others to please some other people. Many actions in interculturality can make use of the strategy of 谗言佞语, whereby one wishes to flatter a person or a group of people by criticizing negatively some other people. Although criticizing others is part of 'human nature' (a lazy and unfair argument, of course!), denigrating some people (e.g. the other, our own people or a 'third' group) for 'seducing', 'complimenting' others, is obviously not an acceptable behaviour. It is interesting though to reflect on why we might be tempted to do so in certain situations. What does it tell about us and about those who listen to us and contribute to such slanders?

USING LANGUAGE IN INTERCULTURALITY

The first section of this chapter focused on problems related to language use that can inspire us to think 'otherwise' in relation to interculturality. In what follows, we examine discourse instruments that suggest ways of thinking about how we can use language to communicate with the other. Translation, as a central theme in interculturality, is also discussed in this section.

信、达、雅—Xìn, dá, yǎ
Can be translated as: *Faithfulness, expressiveness, elegance.*

信 (xìn) means *letter, to trust, to believe, confidence*, with the sub-character for *man* and *person* conveying its meaning; 达 (dá) translates as *to attain, to reach*, and *to communicate*—the sub-character *to walk* conveying its meaning; 雅 (yǎ) is the Chinese word for *elegant*, the sub-character for *a bird* conveys its meaning.

This discourse instrument derives from a translation model put forward by Yan Fu (严复), a thinker and translator of foreign texts (1854–1921). He presented 信、达、雅 as the main challenges of translation, advocating for precision, fluency, clarity and appropriateness when translating into the Chinese language.

As we have seen on several occasions in this book, intercultural communication is mostly about 'translation'. It does not mean that communicating with others requires us to be professional translators/interpreters but that we need to pay attention to word use actively, to critique our ways of translating and handling words in different languages, to translate back, to question the other about their translation and to engage in discussions around faithfulness (understood here as faithfulness to the connotations of words in different contexts), transparency and appropriateness. Without reflecting on translation in interculturality, we miss opportunities for genuine transformation and understanding. This is why we should always bear in mind that a word found in a bilingual dictionary or on Google Translate deserves to be surveyed, discussed, opened up and replaced (should need be). In other words, translate again and again!

格义—*Gé yì*

Can be translated as: *A translation method based on comparison and analogy.*

The discourse instrument of 格义 (gé yì) complements the previous one. 格 (gé, based on the sub-character for *wood* conveying its meaning) translates as *square, style, to investigate, to study exhaustively* and 义 (yì) is the character for *justice, righteousness*, but also *relationship* and *friendship*.

This instrument is derived from a specific method for translating (Indian) Buddhist doctrines into Chinese, when many scriptures were introduced to China in earlier times. In order to make sense of them, vocabulary and formulations from Chinese documents (e.g. Laozi) were borrowed. Matching meanings was then used as a method for translating the doctrines.

格义 also refers to a philosophical concept, whereby comparison and analogy serve the purpose of describing, understanding and explaining a foreign/outsider element. Interculturally what this instrument urges us to do linguistically and conceptually is central to 'getting across' to the other and vice versa. We should bear in mind, however, that 'matching meanings' poses a lot of problems and that we should base this principle on cooperation, revision, and open-mindedness. Making a decision about a specific way of translating, expressing and explaining is somewhat of a partisan decision and thus it requires being transparent and open to change.

微言大义—*Wēi yán dà yì*
Can be translated as: *A profound meaning in subtle words; sublime words with deep meaning.*

微 (wēi) means *tiny, miniature*, but also *to decline* (with the sub-character of to step with the left foot as its radical); 大 (dà) translates as *big, large, huge* and has an ideographic of a man with outstretched arms; finally, 义 (yì) refers to *justice, righteousness* but also *relationship*.

In the instrument, 微言 hints at precise and far-reaching words while 大义 translates as the essence of the Scriptures and the Great Principles. Using a few words to convey deep meaning is another suggested principle for unthinking and rethinking the way we use language in interculturality.

不言之教—*Bù yán zhī jiào*
Can be translated as: *Unspoken teaching; influence others without preaching.*

This discourse instrument is based on four characters, amongst which 之 (zhī, ideographic: a foot meaning to follow) for *him, her, it* and 教 (jiào, the sub-character for *script* conveys its meaning) for *to teach*.

不言之教 is located within the philosophy of 无为 (*wuwei*, early Daoism, see Slingerland, 2003), which refers to *non-action, non-preaching*. One's own behaviours and attitudes, if noble and ethical, are enough as potential examples, to guide others—without us needing to use words to give them 'orders' about what should be done or the kind of behaviours to favour. Objectives for interculturality ('how to behave') are manifold and sometimes expressed and seen differently by people around the world. Opening up to other ways of thinking about it, observing, refraining from judging, and trying to build up new ways of being together, can benefit from 'unspoken teaching'. We need to bear in mind however, that influence must be based on *mutual, joint* transformations of what we do *together*, say *together* and experience *together*, without preaching and giving the impression that the way we see for example, being together is the only acceptable way.

言之无文, 行而不远—*Yán zhī wú wén, xíng ér bù yuǎn*
Can be translated as: *(word-for-word:) Not words, not far; lacklustre wording never travels far; non-elegant words will not become popular.*

言 (yán, ideographic, as a reminder: a tongue sticking out of a mouth) stands for *words, speech, to talk*; 之 (zhī) for *him, her, it*; 无 (wú) translates as *not to have, to lack*; 文 (wén, pictographic: a tattooed chest, representing writing)—a character we have seen on many occasions in the book—translates as *language, culture, writing*; 行 (xíng, ideographic: to take small steps with one's feet) for *to walk, to go, to travel*; 而 (ér) means *and, as well as, but*; 不 (bù) serves as a negative prefix (*not, no*) and 远 (yuǎn, with a sub-character for *walking*) refers to *far, distant* and *remote*.

This discourse instrument is from Confucius and is about the need to be eloquent and convincing in order to achieve our goals. This is useful to reflect on the many situations that one might experience in interculturality, where one's voice is unheard or marginally positioned: we might need to be forceful and persuasive so that others start listening to us and become willing to co-construct ideas and change with us. At the same time, it is important to listen carefully to others to enrich our own ways of thinking, speaking and acting. Triggering interest in what we say is an important aspect of what communication should be about, especially when the focus of a given conversation is meaningful to all.

语不择人—*Yǔ bù zé rén*

Can be translated as: *To speak without looking at the object; to speak what they want and don't care who he/she speaks to and their status in society.*

择 (zé, radical: *the hand*) means *to select, to choose, to differentiate, to eliminate* and 人 (rén) *a person, people.*

This important discourse instrument urges us to speak out, to have the strength and courage to interact with others, regardless of our/their position and status. To dare to speak, to feel one has the power to speak, to be listened to, should be considered as central for interculturality. Perception of power differentials, because of our identity as a member of a specific linguistic, national and/or ethnic group, often prevents us from being willing to or courageous enough to speak. Revising this misconception could make interculturality a much more exciting and forward-looking phenomenon—*interculturality as intercultural!*

人平不语—*Rén píng bù yǔ*

Can be translated as: *If a person is treated fairly and reasonably, they will not express dissatisfaction; (word-for-word translation:) People are silent.*

Beyond the characters for *speech/to talk*, *language* and *people* the discourse instrument includes: 平 for *flat, level, equal, to draw (score)*—ideographic: a levelling scale.

人平不语 refers to situations whereby someone has been treated fairly and thus does not feel the need to complain and express dissatisfaction. We should watch our minds before we speak: Do we really need to share our emotions with others (anger and/or happiness)? How will others feel if they do not share these emotions at the very moment we utter them? Isn't it more important to keep our heart at peace so we do not waste time and energy sharing fleeting sentiments with others and spend quality time with them being and becoming together? In interculturality, before sharing emotions with others, and even before feeling these emotions, there might be a need to look inside our own heart.

你言我语—*Nǐ yán wǒ yǔ*

Can be translated as: *(word-for-word translation:) You speak my language; people talk or argue with each other; when two people communicate together, both sides express their opinions.*

Two characters from this instrument refer to the pronouns *you* / 你 (nǐ) and *I* / 我 (wǒ).

This instrument hints at the importance of people discussing and arguing with each other, letting each other know their points of view. It is through lively conversations, where I say something and you add something, that we can move forward together, change, get closer and 'do' interculturality beyond mere performance. Conversing is based on a constant flow of discourses, words, languaging between people, whereby they agree with each other, contradict each other, complement each other, improve each other and, most importantly… *transform together*. Deep and long-term interaction is the only way *into* the hyphen of the other-self.

Qualifying Language

In this last section, we present discourse instruments of interculturality that can be used to reflect on how we qualify language ('ours' and 'theirs') and on how this promotes but also impedes interculturality.

胡啼番语—*Hú tí fān yǔ*

Can be translated as: *Foreign languages.*

胡 (hú) is a polysemic word which can mean *reckless, outrageous* and refer to *a beard, moustache* and to *non-Han people, especially from Central Asia*; 啼 (tí, composed of a sub-character for *the mouth*) means *to cry, to weep aloud, to hoot*; and 番 (fān, ideographic: sowing seeds on the farm) has to do with *foreign (non-Chinese)*, see *barbarian*. In English, the word *barbarian* comes from Greek *barbaros* for *foreign, strange, ignorant*, based on the root *barbar*, an echoic of indecipherable speech of foreigners.

In the past, 胡啼番语 was a direct reference to foreigners, foreign countries and languages. The way we have perceived others in the past in different parts of the world, through the words we use today, is interesting to reflect on. For example, the word *barbarian*, which was used before in English to refer to 'uncivilized' and 'primitive' others, came from a Greek word, with roots in the Proto-Indo-European language, for someone who spoke a different language, while the idea of the barbarian in China could have more to do with the fact that people were seen as looking different or having specific activities (see the character for *foreign* in Chinese, 番, with the ideographic of sowing seeds on the farm). What we label as *foreign, ethnic, racial*, in different languages needs to be opened up and discussed with others in order to enrich the way we think about interculturality.

艰苦涩滞—*Jiān kǔ sè zhì*

Can be translated as: *Tough and slow; poor language and awkward grammar.*

艰 (jiān) translates as *difficult, hard*; 苦 (kǔ) is for *hardship, pain, to suffer*; 涩 (sè) means *astringent, acerb, hard to understand, obscure*, with an ideographic of water cutting like a knife; 滞 (zhì) means *sluggish*.

This discourse instrument refers to slow and halting speech, having difficulties in expressing one's ideas. It is used to refer to poor grammar and low-level language skills.

Let us reflect for a moment on this instrument. Often, we rush to judge the way people speak a (foreign) language: *their grammar is said to be deficient, their range of vocabularies limited, their expression simplistic* and so on. And, at times, we might even draw biased and unjustified conclusions about their abilities based on these remarks ("they can't think 'properly'; they don't speak 'logically'"). However, we need to reflect more carefully when making such judgements about both the 'quality' of their language use as well as their abilities. For instance, there is no direct link between intelligence, logic and so on, and skills in a foreign language.

What is more, language use is dual, meaning that the way we use a language always relates to the ones we interact with and a given context: if they are willing and supportive, we might feel comfortable speaking with them and thus have more confidence; on the other hand, if they seem unwilling and critical of every word that we say, we will find it difficult to move forward. This is why it is important to open up to the other linguistically (as much as we would expect them to do so) and we should refrain from making quick judgements about them. Interculturality is also about building trust, courage and feelings of being comfortable with each other. 'Slow' language and 'poor' grammar should not be 'brakes' for being and changing together. It is only through practising co-languaging (language-as-co-construction between us) that we will make interculturality a little bit closer to some sort of ideal of togetherness.

花言巧语—*Huā yán qiǎo yǔ*

Can be translated as: *Rhetoric; sweet words; flowery speech; elegant but insincere words.*

Two characters are of interest in this discourse instrument: 花 (huā) for *flower, fancy pattern, lustful*, with an ideographic of a flower in bloom and 巧 (qiǎo), which means *opportunely, skilful,* and contains the sub-character for *work*, conveying its meaning.

花言巧语 refers to deceiving words and artful talk full of cunning statements. As asserted on many occasions in the book, trust is central in interculturality. Depending on our language skills, perceptions of what is honesty/dishonesty, feelings towards a nation, a given individual, we might feel that someone from another place might be trying to deceive us—maybe because we feel that they are using too many 'sweet' words, or maybe because what they say appears to be 'too good to be true'. It is important to reflect on these ideas and thoughts and to question the assumptions they contain. We also need to cooperate with others so they might also revise their own potential biases.

有德者必有言—*Yǒu dé zhě bì yǒu yán*

Can be translated as: *Those who have virtue must have words; virtuous people are sure to write fine works which will be passed onto later generations.*

有 (yǒu, pictophonetic of the moon) means *to have, to be, to exist*; 德 (dé, sub-character for *heart* conveys the meaning) *virtue, goodness, character*; 者 (zhě) refers to *one who (is)*; 必 (bì, sub-character for *heart* conveys the meaning) is *certainly, must, necessarily*; 言 (yán) stands for *words, speech, to say*.

This discourse instrument derives from Confucianism and argues that writers should disseminate moral values through their work. In a similar vein, our own ethics (potentially renegotiated with the other) should guide our intercultural encounters and lead to discussions that make us reflect on what and why we do, think and 'discourse' together with others.

言语道断—*Yán yǔ dào duàn*

Can be translated as: *Meaning is profound and subtle, which can't be expressed in words; we can't solve the problem by talking or negotiating; not relying on words so much.*

The last two characters of this discourse instrument include:

- 道 (dào) for *the path, the road, truth, morality, the Dao* (with *walk* as a sub-character conveying its meaning);
- 断 (duàn) translates as *to break, to cut off, to judge*—ideographic of using an axe to harvest grain.

Related to Buddhism, this instrument reminds us that it is impossible to express the Supreme Truth, which is too profound and delicate to be delineated. It can also refer to not being able to solve a problem through conversation and negotiation. 言语道断 reminds us that there are things that cannot be voiced because of their complexities or our failure at understanding them, while at the same time it urges us to accept the impossibility to solve certain issues when interacting with the other. Although many will find this idea negative and a sign of 'failure' (an ideology which is rejected in many contexts today as we asserted earlier), being unable to communicate around certain aspects that are far too complex, can also represent an opportunity for further discussions, going in directions that one had not considered before and thus considering mutual change in unexpected ways.

语带玄机—*Yǔ dài xuán jī*

Can be translated as: *Language contains profound meaning; language with mystery.*

带 (dài, ideographic: a belt creasing one's robe above but not below) refers to *a belt, a ribbon,* and *to wear, to carry, to raise*; 玄机 (xuán jī; xuán means *black* and *mysterious,* jī is *a machine, an opportunity, flexible,* ideographic: a table made of wood) is *a profound theory in Daoism and Buddhism (mysterious principles).*

This instrument is a reminder that language can contain deep and alternative meanings that need to be reflected upon interculturally. As a reminder of a basic principle of sociality, we agree with Emmanuel Levinas (1998: 111) when he writes, "To meet a man is to be kept awake by an enigma".

临别赠语—*Lín bié zèng yǔ*

Can be translated as: *Farewell message; give words of encouragement or advice respectively at parting.*

This instrument is based on three characters on top of that for *language*: 临 and 别 together (línbié, the ideographic of 别—in English: *to leave, to depart, to classify*—is to draw boundaries between classes) refer to *on parting, facing separation*; 赠 (zèng, based on a sub-character for *money*), is *to give as a present, to repel.*

临别赠语 refers to positive words (e.g. a piece of advice) that one might utter when parting with someone. As a specific process of encounters, interculturality often leads to parting with others, for long- and/or short-term periods. Encouraging each other on parting, based on our mutual learning and change might represent good practice for future reunions.

Pause

Before we summarize the most important points about language from this chapter, let us listen to Canetti (1989: 37):

> More and more frequently I am drawn to examine the words that I carry within myself; they occur to me singly, coming from different languages, and then I wish for nothing more than to reflect on a single such word for a long time. I hold it before me, turn it around; I handle it like a stone, but a marvellous stone, and the earth in which it was embedded is myself.

Canetti captures well what we have attempted to do in this book and the discourse instruments from this chapter show convincingly the importance to include systematically reflections on language in unthinking and rethinking interculturality. Although this is the last thematic chapter of the book, and we might have placed this chapter at the beginning to emphasize the importance of language even more, we believe that leaving the topic to the end, as an encompassing one, sends out an important message.

The chapter started by reminding us of the limits of language and of how it is often misused in communication. Discourse instruments such as "words cannot fully express thought", "Words are not beautiful, words are not believed" or "Summer bugs can't discuss ice" summarize well this painful yet important fact of life.

Some instruments from the chapter also provide guidance for speaking with the other (and vice versa since this is always a two-way process): *To utter words that do not hang together; He who talks too much is prone to make errors; to hurt people in one sentence.* These are simple reminders (sometimes contradictory ones when contrasted) of the simplexity of speaking, reading, listening to people and interacting. They appear simple but they project, in fact, complexity.

An important topic that seems to run through many discourse instruments here is that of being aware of power relations and of the (positive/negative) influence of others: *To speak without looking at the object;*

7 PONDERING OVER LANGUAGE AND INTERCULTURALITY   173

Fig. 7.3 Chapter summary (language and interculturality)

Influence others without preaching; When two people communicate together, both sides express their opinions.

Figure 7.3 summarizes the instruments from the chapter. They are divided up into four categories: the limits of language, misusing language, making use of language for interculturality and characterizing language.

Thinking Further

- Were you aware of the complexities of multilingualism in China before reading the chapter introduction?
- Can you summarize in your own words what you have learnt about the written and spoken forms of the Chinese language while reading the book?
- Reflect on the use of swearwords: How often do you use them in your own language and in other languages? Do you feel comfortable using them? Many people argue that it is easier for them to use swearwords in foreign languages and that they find it liberating to do so. What are your views on this?
- Have you ever been shocked by a foreigner using certain words or phrases in their own language(s), yours and/or a lingua franca? What were they and why?
- For a whole day, note down all examples of situations where you feel you miscommunicated with others? Try to explain and understand why.
- How would you define the idea of *trust*? What does it refer to concretely in intercultural contexts? Is trust a 'universal' idea?
- What are your own stereotypes about how people from other countries might sound like when they speak a global language like English or your own language(s)? Review these elements and reflect on why these ideas have been created.
- What do you make of the instrument asserting, "[language] should be unpretentious and spontaneous while avoiding using an excessive and frivolous style?" Does it make sense to you for interculturality?
- Have you ever reflected on why it is that we are often urged to be successful at 'doing' interculturality and that failure is somewhat avoided as a component of education for interculturality?
- Do you agree that stereotypes are slanders? Balance your arguments.

(*continued*)

(continued)

- You have probably been hurt by someone uttering a stereotype about an aspect of your linguistic identity in the past. Reflect on what happened and how you felt and why. Thinking about this specific occurrence, do you think that stereotypes do contain some 'truth' (as many people would assert)?
- "Intercultural communication is translation, and translation is intercultural communication." Do you share this viewpoint? Explain why (not).
- What would be your own principles for a 'good' translation? In three words, define these principles in a concise manner.
- Discuss this assertion: "Making a decision about a specific way of translating, expressing and explaining is somewhat of a partisan decision and thus it requires being transparent and open to change."
- Could you think of concrete examples of how to perform this principle: "Using a few words to convey deep meaning" (微言大义)?
- How to 'do' 'unspoken teaching' in meaningful ways? Can you think of one example?
- Would you say that this is what interculturality should be about: "It is through lively conversations, where I say something and you add something, that we can move forward together, change, get closer and 'do' interculturality beyond mere performance"?
- How do you translate the word *barbarian* in the different languages that you know? Check the etymologies of these words: What do they tell us about how people saw the other in the past? Do the same exercise with the words *foreign* and *ethnic*.
- If you can speak different languages, do you sometimes feel that people perceive and treat you differently based on your potentially differing skills in these languages?

(*continued*)

(continued)

- Comment on this definition of interculturality from the chapter: "Interculturality requires from those who experience it to look beyond what they (think they) know and to be curious of other types of experiences, feelings, ideologies, meanings and actions, so that their own do not become the gauge for judging others." After reading the chapter, summarize how reflecting systematically on language can contribute to this view of interculturality.

To finish with, the reader will have noted throughout the book that many of the Chinese characters that we have detailed have interesting ideographics or pictographics that can support our reflections on interculturality. Review the ones below and ponder over what new and interesting information you could share with others. Also, try to reflect on these questions: Do you think that such ideographics/pictographics can have an influence on how people perceive the connotations of words? How different would the experience of reading potentially be if the writing system(s) you can read had such extra elements in the representation of words?

- 我 (wǒ): me, I. Ideographic: a hand holding a weapon.
- 己 (jǐ): self, oneself. Pictographic: a loom woven with thread.
- 爱 (ài): to love, to be fond of. Ideographic: to bring a friend into one's house.
- 仁 (rén): humane. Ideographic: a caring relationship between two people.
- 思 (sī): to think, to consider. Ideographic: weighing something with one's mind and heart.
- 多 (duō): many, much, multi-. Ideographic: two nights—that is, many.
- 徒 (tú): disciple, believer, on foot. Ideographic: walking in someone's footsteps.
- 古 (gǔ): ancient, old. Ideographic: words passing through ten mouths.

References

Abdallah-Pretceille, M. (2006). Interculturalism as a Paradigm for Thinking about Diversity. *Intercultural Education, 17*(5), 475–483.
Canetti, E. (1989). *The Secret Heart of the Clock*. Farrar Straus Giroux.
Cheng, A. (2007). *Can China Think?* Seuil/College de France.
Ferri, G. (2018). *Intercultural Communication: Critical Approaches, Future Challenges.* Palgrave Macmillan.
Ibelema, M. (2021). *Cultural Chauvinism: Intercultural Communication and the Politics of Superiority.* Routledge.
Levinas, E. (1998). *Discovering Existence with Husserl.* Northwestern University Press.
Slingerland, E. (2003). *Effortless Action: Wu-wei as Conceptual Metaphor and Spiritual Ideal in Early China.* Oxford University Press.

CHAPTER 8

Interim Conclusions

Fred Dervin

THE TWO-METRE ALLEY

A few days ago, I noticed the title of an event on Chinese social media which read: "新时代英语演讲及写作课程建设与人才培养—English Public Speaking and Writing in the New Era: Course Development and Talent Cultivation". Two phrases caught my attention here 'the New Era' and 'Talent Cultivation'—phrases I have come across repeatedly in English in China, and understood after checking with my Chinese friends a few times what they might mean. Interested to verify what these phrases could mean to non-Chinese speakers, I asked a couple of European friends to speculate about their meanings. As I expected they could not make much sense of the phrases. Interestingly—and tellingly, one of them exclaimed, "I guess they are not meant to mean anything. It is just Chinese propaganda". A long conversation about the idea of *propaganda* followed between us and I wanted us to reflect together with her about why she had this representation of the use of these two phrases in English in the Chinese context. I took the time to show her examples that I had come across in English in 'Western' contexts in recent months, for example, *community engagement*, *Black expressive culture across the Diaspora* and the use of *her/hers, him/her* in email signatures, explaining to her that these were not understood/understandable by many '(non-)Westerners' and that an

© The Author(s), under exclusive license to Springer Nature Switzerland AG 2022
M. Yuan et al., *Change and Exchange in Global Education*, Palgrave Studies on Chinese Education in a Global Perspective,
https://doi.org/10.1007/978-3-031-12770-0_8

179

outsider might also consider them to be mere 'propaganda' or 'politically correct elements'.

This is why joint critical and reflexive initiatives 'digging into' the use of specific phrases, either translated from another *language-thought* (ideologies found in specific uses of language) or extracted from another economic-political context, can help us move beyond judging, misinterpreting while 'massaging' our ideological ego, matter more than ever. Our book represents a stepping-stone for discourses of interculturality in this regard.

I believe that one of the main hurdles to communicating around interculturality (as an object of research and education) globally today relates to the fact that we have built some kind of a wall between us—an ideological, 'guru'-centric, Western centric, monolingual wall—a wall that makes us blind to our own discursive weaknesses.

In Tongcheng City in East China, there is a famous story about an alley dating back to the Qing Dynasty. A Minister originally from this area received a letter from his family one day, asking for a favour. They had argued with their neighbour over the boundary between their houses and a wall that they had constructed to their benefit. They wanted the Minister to intervene. But he declined, claiming that their issue was meaningless in a big world like ours. Upon receiving the letter, they decided to move their wall in order to give more space to their neighbour, thus creating the famous two-metre-wide alley between their houses.

A good lesson for what we are dealing with here: *let's find a way to create an equal alley between glocal perspectives of interculturality.* Following Canetti (1989: 60), this alley must help us achieve the following: "You keep taking note of whatever confirms your ideas—better to write down what refutes and weakens them!". In other words, *Look elsewhere to enrich your own ideas! Acquaint yourselves with ideas you find non-understandable and disturbing at first!*

WHAT IS INTERCULTURAL COMMUNICATION (GLOBAL) EDUCATION ABOUT?

As a specialist of intercultural communication (global) education, people often ask me what is it that I research and lecture about.

Recently one of my interlocutors ventured an answer for me, "Fred, you prepare people to communicate across cultures, right?". I disagreed right away. *I do not and cannot prepare people to 'communicate across cultures*'. This has never been my goal. In English, the verb *To prepare* comes from Latin *praeparare* (i.e. *to make ready beforehand*), from *prae* 'before' + *parare*, 'to make ready'. Considering the complexity, the instability and the 'mystery' of human communication, there is no way that we can be 'prepared beforehand' to meet others (see Dervin & Jacobsson, 2021 on critiques of e.g. the concept of *intercultural competence*). As a human/social being, I can never be sure that my communication with others 'functions' well. I can never be sure that we understand each other. I can never be sure that my words mean the same for other people. And I can never be sure that they 'feel' my words and actions the same way I do.

Intercultural communication is not like a computer programme, whereby, if you know about other 'cultures' and for example, press the right key, you can 'communicate' effectively and successfully.

So, *my work is not and has never been about preparing to communicate.*

At this stage, after 20 years of engagement with the notion of *interculturality*, I would say that what I have been doing myself and together with colleagues from around the world, and recently with my Chinese co-authors, is to *unthink and rethink our encounters*. The word *encounter* in English has an interesting etymology. Borrowed from old French *encontrer*, *to encounter* first had the meaning of *to confront, to fight, to oppose* (*counter* is from Latin *contra* for *against*). Today, the phrase *intercultural encounters*, together with other expressions such as *intercultural dialogue*, *intercultural exchange*, is much more positive. Today's French for encounter is *rencontrer*, an *r-* to the original *encontrer* was added to the word, as if to indicate that every time we meet someone, we encounter *again* or *afresh, anew*.

I think that this is what interculturality is about: *we always meet again, afresh* and *anew*. When I encounter someone, we need to start afresh. This idea is actually reflected in the keyword of *interculturality*, as has been mentioned again and again in this book: the root *inter-* indicates reciprocity, in-betweenness while *-ality* hints at a never-ending process, a lifelong endeavour. Going back to the argument from the beginning of this section (we cannot prepare to communicate across cultures), this now makes sense: the *never-ending process of in-betweenness* is far too complex to prepare for beforehand.

This idea may sound disappointing and demotivating to many readers. However, let me now say a few words about my idea of *unthinking and rethinking our encounters* and why I feel it is a powerful way to deal with interculturality.

In this book, we have examined over 50 'Chinese' discourse elements concerning the following central aspects of interculturality:

- Approaching interculturality: Culture and civilization as discursive and reflexive tools (Chap. 2);
- Exploring and explaining experiences of interculturality (Chap. 3);
- 'Doing' interculturality together (Chap. 4);
- Making interculturality work together, as group/community members (Chap. 5);
- Learning to 'do' interculturality—*Setting objectives for oneself* (Chap. 6);
- Pondering over language and interculturality (Chap. 7).

Each chapter forces us to ask ourselves many questions when we meet the other, without really providing answers—just suggestions. For anthropologist Claude Levi-Strauss (1964: 71), "The scientific mind does not so much provide the right answers as ask the right questions." Identifying and asking 'right' questions is the key to reflecting on our *encounters*. For example, have you ever thought about why you see the world, yourself and other people in certain ways? Who has influenced you in doing so? Also, how the way we have been made to look at the world, self and other people influences how we encounter each other? The question, "*How ready are we to look at the world, self and other people differently*"? is also an important one, I believe; and this book should serve as a mirror for self and other to look into our realities and accept change in perspectives when we meet and negotiate meanings.

The way I was made to think about China through my education, academia, the (social) media I have consulted, my parents and friends, advertising, but also my limited linguistic world (I only know so-called 'Indo-European languages') have actually prevented me from encountering Chinese people (and others) in ways that reflect more complex realities.

Let me give you some examples.

When I visited Hetian in Xinjiang (Western part of China), a conversation with the city mayor about Gēzi xiàng (鸽子巷, 'Dove lane', where people used to trade doves) in the old town Tuancheng, reminded me of the importance of unthinking and rethinking the way one sees and talks about the world—*as scholars, educators and individuals*. Stunned by the beauty of the buildings I congratulated the mayor for the recent renovations. Walking down the long lane, I had noticed many similarities with Venice, Italy. I told the mayor: "Hetian is like the Venice of China—without the water!". Amused by the comment—which I thought would please him—the mayor responded, "What if Venice is the Hetian of Europe?". I was stunned. *He hit the nail on the head!* I had come to Hetian with my own "formulas", my ignorance and consequent 'Eurocentrism'. More importantly, as a scholar, I had forgotten to *let my mind watch itself,* to borrow a phrase from Albert Camus (2008: 125).

My limited linguistic world has also often prevented me from encountering others with a critical, reflexive and open mind. Working on this book with my co-authors, I came across a long list of words in English, which I never questioned, assuming they meant and connoted the same way for all. I could take as an example the very word Minzu in Chinese, which is often mistranslated in English as *ethnicity* and even *nationality* (I have also seen the concept of 'race' being used for it!). In the Indo-European languages that I know, the equivalents to the English words can hint at different things, and depending on the context, they can bring to mind different images, different realities and different ideologies. So, mistranslating Minzu in English, without reflecting on the connotations of the translation of the word, and ignoring and being unaware of the specificities of the Chinese context in relation to Minzu, will play against encountering other people. Now that I have been working with my co-authors on Minzu and intercultural education for several years, the more sophisticated understanding of the notion and of the Chinese context that I have developed together with them, allows me to encounter Chinese colleagues and friends in a somewhat more mature way—while remaining modest about this assertion. As Gluck puts it (2009: 20), "As words change, the world changes". After working on this book, I do believe that translating words (and thus actions) again and again does contribute to encounter better.

CHINESE STORIES ARE GLOBAL AND LOCAL

By reviewing and discussing over 50 instruments, we took a trip through Chinese history of thought, Chinese diversity, encounters between China and the world, today's political and ideological Chinese spheres. The insights shared on both Chinese and English (e.g. etymology, ideographics) remind us of the importance to play the 'archaeologist' to get a fuller sense of what words used for interculturality hint at. Jean Cocteau's (1968: 8) comparison of every poem to *a coat of arms* is a stimulating metaphor for working on interculturality: "It [the poem] must be deciphered. How much blood, how many tears in exchange for these axes, these muzzles, these unicorns, these torches, these towers, these martlets, these seedlings of stars and these fields of blue!".

This book reminds us that interculturality is first and foremost about humanity. Chinese stories are also very much global stories in that sense. They tell us about our connected humanity, *our similarities* and *differences*. The different chapters force us to open our ears and our eyes (amongst others) in front of the diverse ways of thinking about interculturality and to unthink and rethink 'our' own. *Diverse* here does not necessarily mean *different*. As we have seen many times in the book, some Chinese discourse instruments have (direct) equivalents in other parts of the world. Sometimes it takes time to realize that we do have similarities in differences and vice versa. Finally, some of the ideas from 'Chinese stories of interculturality' may not always sound novel, however, following Canetti (1989: 95), we could argue that "It does not matter how new an idea is: what matters is how new it becomes."

Repeating the same ideas about interculturality, rehearsing imposed ideologies from a selected few 'Western' scholars, using trendy English words to talk about the notion, represent threats since these provide researchers and educators with limited questions and answers globally. Interculturality should serve the purpose of providing educators and students with 气质 (Qìzhí), a Chinese word for vital/renewed energy—here: the curiosity to move forward in our thinking, over and over, without ever being satisfied with what we do, find and obtain!

再见

Some words of temporary conclusions. During a recent panel discussion around the concept of 'global competence in education', I was asked the following two questions. We were finishing this book when I gave the talk and it inspired most of my answers:

1. **"What recommendations would you have for schools to develop students' global/intercultural competence?"**

- Provide opportunities for students to negotiate together what they could be expected to learn 'globally' when working together—rather than adults pushing some 'orders' onto them;
- Make the students do something meaningful together that will allow them to explore their differences AND similarities;
- Allow them to reflect on how their own contexts influence the way they see global/intercultural competence and learn about other ways of reflecting on the competence;
- Guide them in learning to listen to others (rather than merely 'hearing' them) and to reflect on the 'flavours' of the words they use in different languages and English as a lingua franca. Learning to listen to other people, to take the time to listen to them and to find the motivation to do so, should be the core of education today. If we don't listen, our encounters will be unequal, mere performances… *inauthentic encounters.*
- Guide them in learning to listen to themselves and to reflect on why they refuse, condemn, judge, accept certain ways of being, doing, living and so on. Remember the phrase I borrowed from Camus (2008: 125) earlier: *we must let our 'mind watch itself'!* What we think we know about other people—and at the same time about ourselves—is not always the *only reality.* We encounter each other through 'images of images of images' and we must thus learn to deconstruct these images.

2. **"How to move global competence from awareness to practice?"**

Always bear in mind:

- **The Economic-political-ideological positions** of the one who talks about global/intercultural competence;
- **The untranslatability** of the words we use to talk about interculturality, which need to be translated again and again in English as a global language and other languages;
- **Big-hearted generosity**: listen to what others have to say about global/intercultural competence and to how they formulate it. Learn *with* them about it and refuse one single 'order' to do global/intercultural competence. Not a single individual or institution knows really, what it is about. In a sense, we all know what it is, in our own and, often, similar ways.

The word 再见 (zài jiàn) means *good bye* in Chinese. Like French *au revoir*, it translates word-for-word as 'see again' (compare to English: *goodbye* is a contraction of *God be with you*). This book follows the publication of several volumes written together with Yuan, Sude and Chen, and concluding this new one we do not say *goodbye* but 再见 (see again). We have experienced very unstable times since 2020 but, to finish on a forward-looking note, let us remember to dream of a new world of interculturality in global education and to listen to as many new stories as possible.

References

Camus, A. (2008). *Notebooks 1951-1959*. Ivan Dee.
Canetti, E. (1989). *The Secret Heart of the Clock*. Farrar Straus Giroux.
Cocteau, J. (1968). *Two Screenplays: The Blood of a Poet and The Testament of Orpheus*. Orion Press.
Dervin, F., & Jacobsson, A. (2021). *Teacher Education for Critical and Reflexive Interculturality*. Palgrave Macmillan.
Gluck, C. (2009). Words in Motion. In C. Gluck & A. Lowenhaupt Tsing (Eds.), *Words in Motion: Toward a Global Lexicon* (pp. 20–36). Duke University Press.
Levi-Strauss, C. (1964). *The Raw and the Cooked*. Chicago University Press.

Full List of Discourse Instruments

Chapter 2

Approaching Interculturality: Culture, Civilization and Identity as Discursive and Reflexive Tools

文化自觉—Wén huà zì jué (Cultural self-awareness).
文化翻译—Wén huà fān yì (Cultural translation, cultural awareness).
文化素质—Wén huà sù zhì (Cultural/inner quality, cultural competence, education).
文化修养—Wén huà xiū yǎng (Cultural cultivation, accomplishment or even self-cultivation).
文化主体性—Wén huà zhǔ tǐ xìng (Cultural subjectivity).
文化基因—Wén huà jī yīn (Cultural gene).
文化常识—Wén huà cháng shí (Cultural commonsense, cultural literacy, cultural knowledge and Chinese culture).
文化归属感—Wén huà guī shǔ gǎn (A cultural (sense of) belonging).
动静—Dòng jìng (Sign of activity, movement and stillness).
变化—Biàn huà (Variety, change).
发展—Fā zhǎn (Development, progress, change).
提高全民文明素质、文化素质—Tí gāo quán mín wén míng sù zhì, wén huà sù zhì (Improve education on culture, civility and arts (Improve the civilized and cultural qualities of all people).

改造落后的文化—Gǎi zào luò hòu de wén huà (To transform a backward culture).
人文交流—Rén wén jiāo liú (Cultural and people-to-people exchange).
文化词汇—Wén huà cí huì (Culture-loaded words/cultural vocabulary).
文化底蕴—Wén huà dǐ yùn (Cultural deposits, cultural heritage).
文化创新—Wén huà chuàng xīn (Cultural innovation).
文化本土化—Wén huà běn tǔ huà (Cultural localization).
文化建设—Wén huà jiàn shè (Cultural construction).
文化强国—Wén huà qiáng guó (A culturally strong country).
文化输出—Wén huà shū chū (Cultural output).
文化复兴—Wén huà fù xīng (Cultural renaissance, revival).
文化折扣—Wén huà zhé kòu (Cultural discount).
文化污染—Wén huà wū rǎn (Cultural pollution, Unhealthy spiritual and cultural products).
旅游美时美刻，文明随时随地—Lǚ yóu měi shí měi kè, wén míng suí shí suí dì (Behave politely on vacation, civilization will show; (word-for-word) Travel is beautiful in time, civilization is anytime, anywhere).
文明是最美的风景—Wén míng shì zuì měi de fēng jǐng (Civilization is the most beautiful scenery).
旅途漫漫，文明相伴—Lǚ tú màn màn, wén míng xiāng bàn (Bring civilization with long journey, (word-for-word translation) Long journey, accompanied by civilization).
讲文明话办文明事做文明人·创文明城—Jiǎng wén míng huà, bàn wén míng shì, zuò wén míng rén, chuàng wén míng chéng (Speak civilized words, do civilized things, be civilized people, create a civilized city).
文化衫—Wén huà shān (DIY/cultural T-shirt).
文化创意产业—Wén huà chuàng yì chǎn yè (Cultural and Creative Industries (CCI)).
文化名片—Wén huà míng piàn (Cultural name card).
汉服文化—Hàn fú wén huà (Hanfu culture).
红色文化—Hóng sè wén huà (Red culture).

Chapter 3

Exploring and Explaining Experiences of Interculturality

文化自大—Wén huà zì dà (Cultural arrogance).
外国的月亮比中国的圆—Wài guó de yuè liàng bǐ zhōng guó de yuan (The foreign moon is rounder than the Chinese moon).
文化渗透—Wén huà shèn tòu (Cultural infiltration, penetration, but also, cross-fertilization of culture).
文化入侵—Wénhuà rùqīn (Cultural invasion/aggression).
文化竞争力—Wén huà jìng zhēng lì (Cultural competitiveness).
文化强国—Wénhuà qiángguó (Cultural power).
文化软实力—Wén huà ruǎn shí lì (Cultural soft power).
十年树木，百年树人—Shí nián shù mù, bǎinián shù rén (It takes ten years to grow trees, but a hundred to rear people).
多元化—Duōyuán huà (Pluralism, diversification, multiculturalism).
异境茫然—Yì jìng máng rán (Change of scenery, depaysement, disorientation).
四海为家—Sìhǎi wéi jiā (To regard the four corners of the world all as home).
入境问俗—Rù jìng wèn sú (Enter the realm of other countries, first ask about their ban; When entering the capitals of other countries, ask their customs first).
潜移默化—Qiányímòhuà (Imperceptibly, silent transformations, unknowingly changing).
不识庐山真真面目，只缘身在此山中—Lú shān zhēn miàn mù (I see not the true face of Mount Lushan as I am right in it).
张飞穿针 - 粗中有细—Zhāng fēi cìzhēn cūxì (Zhang Fei piercing needle—thick but thin).
井里的蛤蟆-没见过大天—Jǐng lǐ de hámá-méi jiàn guo dà tiān (A frog in a well—never having seen the whole sky).
尊重—Zūn zhòng (Respect, value; to esteem; to respect; to honor; to value; eminent; serious; proper).
尊敬—Zūn jìng (To respect; to revere).
会心—Huì xīn (Understanding each other without words. Heart-to-heart communication).
人同此心，心同此理—Rén tóng cǐ xīn, xīn tóng cǐ lǐ (Empathy, people have the same heart, the heart has the same reason).

尺有所短, 寸有所长—Chǐ yóu suǒ duǎn, cùn yóu suǒ cháng (A foot may prove short while an inch may prove long; everyone has their weak and strong points).

尽信书, 不如无书—Jìn xìn shū, bùrú wú shū (It is better to believe in books than to have no books; be critical of what you read).

Chapter 4

'Doing' Interculturality Together

非攻—Fēi gong (Opposing and denouncing unjust warfare, non-attack).

协和万邦—Xié hé wàn bāng (Harmonious coexistence of all).

有容乃大—Yǒu róng nǎi dà (Tolerance is a virtue; accommodate others; a broad mind achieves greatness).

和谐—Hé xié (Harmony).

以和为贵—Yǐ hé wéi guì (Harmony is the most precious; harmony is to be prized).

美美与共—Měi měi yǔ gong (A diversified and harmonious world).

君子和而不同, 小人同而不和—Jūn zǐhé ér bù tóng, xiǎo rén tóng ér bù hé (Gentlemen respect each other although they may disagree).

投桃报李—Tóu táo bào lǐ (Mutual courtesy).

兼爱—Jiān ài (Universal love).

四海—Sìhǎi (The four seas or the entire world).

十里不同俗—Shílǐ bùtóng sú (Other countries, other manners; ten miles is different).

各美其美, 美人之美, 美美与共, 天下大同—Gè měi qí měi, měirén zhīměi, měiměi yǔgòng, tiānxià dàtóng (Appreciate the culture/values of others as do to one's own, and the world will become a harmonious whole; everybody cherishes his or her own culture/values, and if we respect and treasure other's culture/values, the world will be a harmonious one (word-for-word translation: each has its own beauty, the beauty of the beauty, the beauty of the same, the world is the same).

兼听—Jiān tīng (Listening to a variety of voices, to others; listening to opinions widely).

道不同, 不相为谋—Dào bùtóng, bù xiāng wéi móu (Persons who walk different paths cannot make plans/work together).

正名(辨正名称、名分, 使名实相副)—Zhèngmíng (biànzhèng míngchēng, míng fèn, shǐ míng shí xiāng fù) (Rectification of names;

to replace the current name or title of something with a new one that reflects its true nature; to make a name match the reality).

合同异—Hé tóng yì (Unify/combine similarity and difference).

大同而与小同异，此之谓 "小同异"。万物毕同毕异，此之谓"大同异"—Dà tóng ér xiǎo tóng yì, cǐzhī wèi " xiǎo tóng yì". wàn wù bì tóng bì yì, cǐzhī wèi "dà tóng yì" (Minor commonality and differentiation; similarity and small differences refer to roughly the same with slight differences).

庄周梦蝶—Zhuāng zhōu mèng dié (Relative difference between all things is needed).

道通为一—Dào tōng wéi yī (Opposite things complement each other).

兵强则灭—Bīng qiáng zé miè (Everything has two sides; word-for-word translation: if the soldiers are strong, they will die).

同归殊途—Tóng guī shū tú (Same destination but different routes; same goal, different ways).

见贤思齐焉, 见不贤而内自省也—Jiàn xián sī qí yān, jiàn bù xián ér nèi zìxǐng yě (When one meets a virtuous person, one should consider learning from them; if one sees an immoral person, one should introspect to avoid being immoral).

教学相长—Jiào xué xiāng zhǎng (Teaching and learning promote each other).

结拜—Jié bài (Sworn brothers or sisters).

相辅相成—Xiāng fǔ xiāng chéng (Supplement and complement each other).

知行合一—Zhī xíng hé yī (You learn something, you act upon it; knowledge and action should go hand in hand, knowledge is action, action is knowledge).

视人如己—Shì rén rú jǐ (Treat/see others as yourself).

礼尚往来—Lǐshàngwǎnglái (Reciprocity as a social norm, proper behavior is based on reciprocity, to return politeness for politeness).

管鲍之交—Guǎn bào zhī jiāo (Friendship between Guan and Bao; as Close as Guan Zhong and Bao Shuya; David and Jonathan).

己所不欲，勿施于人—Jǐ suǒ bù yù, wù shī yú rén (Do unto others as you would have them do unto you; what you don't want done to you, don't do to others).

三人行，必有我师焉—Sān rénxíng, bì yǒu wǒ shī (When three people walk together, there must be someone worth imitating).

Chapter 5

Making Interculturality Work Together, as Group/Community Members

民族—**Mín zú** (Ethnic (group), nation(ality), Minzu (preferred)).
民族团结—**Mín zú tuán jié** (National unity, ethnic solidarity, ethnic harmony).
中华民族多元一体化—**Zhōng huá mín zú duō yuán yī tǐ huà** (plural unity pattern, pluralistic unity, the Chinese nation is pluralistic and unified).
中华民族共同体意识—**Zhōng huá mín zú gòng tóng tǐ yì shí** (The sense of community of the Chinese nation).
优惠政策—**Yōu huì zhèng cè** (Preferential policies).
一带一路—**Yī dài yī lù** (One Belt One Road).
人类命运共同体—**Rén lèi mìng yùn gòng tóng tǐ** (A community with a shared future for mankind).
上海精神—**Shànghǎi jīngshén** (Shanghai spirit).
石榴同心—**Shí liu tóng xīn** (United closely as seeds of a pomegranate).
大杂居小聚居—**Dà zá jū xiǎo jù jū** (Minzu groups live with each other, while some live in concentrated communities; (word-for-word translation:) large mixed living and small living together).
一体多元—**Yī tǐ duō yuan** (United but pluralistic; (word-for-word translation:) 'one multi-dimensional').
民族情怀—**Mín zú qíng huái** (Minzu feelings/sentiment; the passion and beloved feelings for all Minzu groups in China).
精神相依—**Jīng shén xiāng yī** (People from Minzu groups rely on each other's spirit; (word-for-word translation:) spiritual interdependence).
天下乃天下之天下—**Tiānxià nǎi tiānxià zhī tiānxià** (The world is the world of the world; all under heaven belongs to the people).
海内存知己，天涯诺比邻—**Hǎi nèi cún zhī jǐ, tiān yá ruò bǐ lín** (The sea is an intimate friend/a confident, the world is close by).
唇亡齿寒—**Chúnwángchǐhán** (Lips and teeth are cold; once the lips are gone, the teeth will feel cold; intimately interdependent; close partners).
你中有我，我中有你—**Nǐ zhōng yǒu wǒ, wǒ zhōng yǒu nǐ** (You have me, I have you; there is me in you and you in me).
求大同存小异—**Qiú dàtóng cún xiǎo yì** (Seek common ground while reserving differences; seek common ground and small differences).

手足情深—Shǒu zú qíng shēn (People get along very well like Castor and Pollux; the love between brothers is deep; brotherhood).
亲诚惠容—Qīn chéng huì róng (Sincerely welcome; inclusiveness).
人心归聚—Rén xīn jù guī (People come together).
怀远以德—Huái yuǎn yǐ dé (Embrace/respect distant peoples by means of virtue).
守望相助—Shǒu wàng xiāng zhù (To keep watch and defend one another; to join forces to defend against external aggressors; mutual help and protection).
吸收外国文化有益成果—Xī shōu wài guó wén huà yǒu yì chéng guǒ (Absorbing the good sides of foreign cultures).
他山之石，可以攻玉—Tā shān zhī shí, kěyǐ gōng yù (Stones from other mountains/hills can serve to polish jade).
多元一体教育—Duō yuán yī tǐ jiào yù (Multi-in-one education; multi-integrated, multicultural education; Minzu education).
民族团结教育—Mín zú tuán jié jiāo yù (Education for Minzu unity).
双语教育—Shuāng yǔ jiāo yù (Bilingual education).
增进共同性、尊重和包容差异性—Zēng jìn gòng tóng xìng, zūn zhòng hé bāo róng chā yì xìng (Promote commonality, respect and tolerance of differences).

Chapter 6

Learning to 'Do' Interculturality: **Setting Objectives for Oneself**

君子—Jūn zǐ (Man of virtue; person of noble character; nobleman).
仁者爱人—Rén zhě ài rén (A benevolent person loves others; the benevolent person has a loving heart).
反求诸己—Fǎn qiú zhū jǐ (Turn inward and examine yourself when you encounter difficulties in life; to seek the cause in oneself rather than in somebody else; to think behind closed curtains; moral cultivation).
怨天尤人—Yuàn tiān yóu rén (To complain against heaven and bear a grudge against men; to blame the gods and accuse others).
三省吾身—Sān xǐng wú shēn (Reflect on oneself several times a day; introspection).
知常达变—Zhī cháng dá biàn (Know how to change; be aware of change; master both permanence and change).

修己安人—Xiū jǐ ān rén (Cultivate oneself to benefit others; self-cultivation; self-betterment).

爱人为大—Ài rén wéi dà (Love people; being caring for people; caring for Others is the priority.)

礼—Lǐ (rites, norms, manners, respectful attitude, ceremony or Li).

换位思考—Huàn wèi sī kǎo (To put yourself in the other person's shoes; mutual empathy and understanding; perspective taking).

推己及人—Tuī jǐ jí rén (self-cultivation; putting oneself in another's place).

恕—Shù (Being considerate; to show forgiveness).

水至清则无鱼, 人至察则无徒—Shuǐ zhì qīng zé wú yú, rén zhì chá zé wú tú (There is no fish when the water is too clear; one should not set the bar too high for a person).

己所不欲, 勿施于人—Jǐ suǒ bù yù, wù shī yú rén (Do not do unto others, do not impose on others).

不置褒贬—Bù zhì bāo biǎn (Passing no judgement on; neither praising nor criticizing).

转益多师—Zhuǎn yì duō shī (Learn from many masters, form your own style).

众盲摸象—Zhòng máng mō xiàng (Blindly touch the elephant; multitude of blind people touch an elephant; unable to see the big picture; to mistake the part for the whole).

齐物—Qí wù (Seeing things as equal; reconciling differences and contradictions among things).

鉴古知今—Jiàn gǔ zhī jīn (Learn from the past and study the present; review the past to understand the present).

读万卷书, 行万里路—Dú wàn juàn shū, xíng wàn lǐ lù (Read more walk more; read ten thousand books and travel ten thousand Li, but also, Learn as much as you can and do all you can).

君子不器—Jūn zǐ bù qì (A gentleman is not an implement/a vessel).

日新月异—Rì xīn yuè yì (Constant renewal; every day sees new developments; rapid progress).

满招损, 谦受益—Mǎn zhāo sǔn, qiān shòu yì (Complacency leads to failure, modesty to success; conceit and complacency cause failure whereas modesty and prudence bring success).

虚一而静—Xū yī ér jìng (Void and quiet; open-mindedness, concentration and tranquility).

慎思明辨—Shèn sī míng biàn (Think carefully and discern; careful reflection and clear discrimination).

三思而行—Sān sī ér xíng (Taking action after having reflected several times; think thrice before acting; don't act before you've thought it through carefully).
实事求是—Shí shì qiú shì (Seek truth from facts; to be practical and realistic).

Chapter 7

Reflecting on Language and Interculturality

言不尽意—Yán bù jìn yì (Words cannot fully express thought; words don't exhaust ideas; to speak with reticence).
言高语低—Yán gāo yǔ dī (High talk and low talk; to speak inconsequently and without discretion).
前言不搭后语—Qián yán bù dā hòu yǔ (To utter words that do not hang together; can't connect back and forth; to talk/speak incoherently; also, self-contradictory).
修辞立诚—Xiūcí lìchéng (Rhetorical and honest; to establish credibility through careful choice of words; rhetoric is sincere).
信言不美，美言不信—Xìn yán bù měi, měi yán bù xìn (Words are not beautiful, words are not believed; trustworthy words may not be fine-sounding; fine-sounding words may not be trustworthy).
语焉不详—Yǔ yān bù xiáng (Speak and communicate superficially; not to speak in details).
言多语失—Yán duō yǔ shī (He who talks too much is prone to make errors; if one says too much, one is bound to slip up at some point).
夏虫不可以语冰—Xià chóng bù kě yǐ yǔ bīng (Summer bugs can't see/discuss ice; short-sighted without understanding the truth).
一语中人—Yī yǔ zhòng rén (Hurt people in one sentence; slander).
谗言佞语—Chán yán nìng yǔ (Words that slander others and flatter others).
信、达、雅—Xìn, dá, yǎ (Faithfulness, expressiveness, elegance).
格义—Gé yì (A translation method based on comparison and analogy).
微言大义—Wēi yán dà yì (A profound meaning in subtle words; sublime words with deep *meaning*.
不言之教—Bù yán zhī jiào (Unspoken teaching; influence others without preaching).

言之无文，行而不远—Yán zhī wú wén, xíng ér bù yuǎn (word-for-word:) Not words, not far; lackluster wording never travels far; non-elegant words will not become popular.

语不择人—Yǔ bù zé rén (To speak without looking at the object; to speak what they want and don't care who he/she speak to and their status in society).

人平不语—Rén píng bù yǔ If a person is treated fairly and reasonably, they will not express dissatisfaction; (word-for-word translation:) People are silent.

你言我语—Nǐ yán wǒ yǔ (word-for-word translation:) You speak my language; people talk or argue with each other; when two people communicate together, both sides express their opinions.

胡啼番语—Hú tí fān yǔ (Foreign languages).

艰苦涩滞—Jiān kǔ sè zhì (Tough and slow; poor language and awkward grammar).

花言巧语—Huā yán qiǎo yǔ (Rhetoric; sweet words; flowery speech; elegant but insincere words).

有德者必有言—Yǒu dé zhě bì yǒu yán (Those who have virtue must have words; virtuous people are sure to write fine works which will be passed on to later generations).

言语道断—Yán yǔ dào duàn (Meaning is profound and subtle, which can't be expressed in words; we can't solve the problem by talking or negotiating; not relying on words so much).

语带玄机—Yǔ dài xuán jī (Language contains profound meaning; language with mystery).

临别赠语—Lín bié zèng yǔ (Farewell message; give words of encouragement or advice respectively at parting).

Index[1]

A
All under heaven, 111, 112, 192
Arrogance, 18, 21, 41, 56–58, 71, 73, 189
Awareness, 7, 29, 30, 32, 40, 42, 49, 56, 72, 105, 185, 187

B
Beautiful, 2, 11, 13, 43, 44, 61, 64, 81, 84, 89, 127, 134, 160, 172, 188, 195
Beauty, 13, 58, 81, 84, 86, 89, 96, 183, 190
Benevolence, 129, 134, 144
Bilingual education, 118, 120, 193
Brotherhood, 92, 114, 120, 158, 193

C
Change, 9, 17–21, 28, 32, 34–37, 39, 40, 49, 50, 55, 59, 60, 64–67, 86–91, 96, 99, 101, 103, 105, 114, 117, 127, 131–135, 138, 140–143, 145, 147, 149, 150, 161, 164, 166, 167, 170, 171, 175, 182, 183, 187, 189, 193
Chinese Dream (the), 63, 106, 110
Civilization, 15, 19, 20, 22, 25–52, 79, 100, 105, 116, 182, 187–188
Coexistence, 77, 78, 80, 86, 109, 123, 190
Communication, 1, 5n2, 10, 11, 38, 56–63, 70, 94, 119, 158, 160, 164, 166, 172, 175, 180–183, 189
Community, 20, 34, 101–124, 179, 182, 192–193

---

[1] Note: Page numbers followed by 'n' refer to notes.

© The Author(s), under exclusive license to Springer Nature Switzerland AG 2022
M. Yuan et al., *Change and Exchange in Global Education*, Palgrave Studies on Chinese Education in a Global Perspective,
https://doi.org/10.1007/978-3-031-12770-0

198 INDEX

Community with a shared future for mankind, 107, 114, 192
Competence, 7, 17, 30, 49, 51, 181, 184, 185, 187
Cooperation, 1, 15, 20, 29, 66, 80, 91, 107–110, 113, 157, 164
Cosmopolitan, 65, 84
Culturalism, 138
Culture, 5, 6, 12, 14, 15, 18, 19, 21, 22, 25–52, 56–64, 67, 72, 81, 84, 100, 103, 105, 106, 116–118, 122, 138, 145, 150, 155, 166, 179–182, 187–190, 193
Curiosity, 13, 16, 42, 66, 138, 141, 184

D

Depaysement, 10n3, 64, 189
Development, 22, 29, 35, 37, 39, 42, 50, 52, 68, 102, 104, 106, 108–110, 117, 123, 141, 187, 194
Dialect/dialects, 12, 58, 118, 132, 154, 155, 158
Dialogue, 10, 39, 56, 66, 71, 181
Difference, 5n2, 7, 12, 18, 20, 30, 70, 77, 80, 84, 87–91, 96, 103, 105, 114, 119, 120, 122, 133, 139, 145, 155, 184, 185, 191–194
Differilitude/differilitudes, 70, 96, 102
Diversity, 3, 4, 7, 11, 15, 16n5, 52, 64, 66, 78, 81, 90, 96, 106, 109, 118, 123, 145, 183

E

Education, 1, 2, 4, 7, 9, 13, 16, 17, 19–21, 25, 28, 30, 32, 36, 49, 57, 60, 65, 78, 98, 101, 104, 117, 118, 120, 122, 123, 125, 128, 145, 150, 151, 174, 180–187, 193
Empathy, 70, 72, 134–136, 144, 148, 189, 194
English, 2, 4, 5n2, 6, 7, 10, 10n3, 14, 18, 19, 21, 25–32, 34, 35, 37, 39, 40, 42–44, 46, 49, 57, 60, 61, 63–65, 67, 69, 70, 74, 79–81, 83, 86–88, 90, 91, 94, 97, 98, 101–103, 105–109, 111, 115, 119, 127, 128, 131, 132, 134, 135, 139, 141, 143, 145, 149, 155, 159, 162, 168, 171, 174, 179, 181, 183–186
Equality, 36, 50, 79, 83, 90, 104, 108, 110, 115, 118, 123, 137
Essentialism, 41
Ethnocentrism, 57
Etymology, 19, 86, 101, 122, 127, 162, 175, 181, 183

F

Flatter, 163, 195
Flavours (of words), 14, 69, 185

G

Generosity, 137, 185
Glocal, 81, 120, 180
Golden Rule, 95, 137, 150
Great Harmony, 114, 123

H

Hanfu, 46, 48, 188
Happiness, 45, 60, 110, 111, 123, 167
Harmony, 20, 29, 70, 77, 79–88, 96, 97, 103, 119, 127, 190, 192

INDEX 199

I
Identity, 6, 19, 28–37, 48, 50, 51, 56, 58, 94, 101, 106, 145, 150, 153, 155, 158, 162, 166, 175, 187–188
Ideology/ideologies, 2n1, 4, 5n2, 6–9, 15, 32, 37, 50, 52, 56, 61, 65, 78, 94, 102, 142, 162, 170, 176, 180, 183, 184
Infiltration, 59, 72, 189
Introspection, 91, 131, 136, 149, 193

J
Jūnzǐ, 81, 98, 127, 144, 145, 149

L
Language, 2, 6, 8, 10–21, 10n3, 27, 30, 31, 37, 38, 42, 43, 46, 49, 51, 56, 58, 60, 63, 69, 83, 87, 97, 98, 100–103, 108, 109, 117–119, 122–124, 128, 132, 139, 150, 153–176, 180, 182, 183, 185, 195–196
Learning, 9, 13, 14, 16, 20, 31, 63, 64, 66, 74, 91–96, 99, 102, 107, 117–119, 121, 125–151, 171, 182, 185, 191, 193–195
Li, 126, 133, 140, 194

M
MacDonaldization, 59
Mandarin, 12, 119, 154, 155
Mélange, 11, 59, 117, 139
Metaphor, 2, 3, 5n2, 7, 8, 21, 43, 67, 68, 71, 109, 120, 122, 126, 140, 162, 184
Minzu, 5, 6, 11, 36, 81, 92, 102–104, 106, 109, 110, 117–120, 122, 155, 183, 192, 193

Minzu education, 117, 119, 120, 193
Mirror, 14, 17, 56, 58, 68, 91, 126, 139, 144, 182
Mixing, 32, 59, 117
Moderation, 34, 137, 161
Movement, 4, 34, 35, 50, 52, 59, 187
Multicultural education, 117, 120, 193
Multilingual, 5n2, 69
Mutuality, 96, 110

N
Nationalism, 58, 61
Non-violence, 77, 78

O
One Belt One Road, 107, 123, 192
Open-minded, 84, 115
Opposites, 89, 99, 130, 139, 159, 160, 162, 191

P
Perception/perceptions, 31, 67, 133, 166, 169
Permanence, 131, 132, 149, 193
Politics, 72, 101, 106, 108, 122
Pomegranate, 108, 109, 122, 192
Preferential policies, 106, 119, 123, 192
Prosperity, 79, 104, 109, 110

R
Reciprocity, 20, 69, 77, 83, 91–96, 99, 110, 113, 122, 130, 137, 149, 181, 191
Reflexivity, 16, 20, 96, 120, 125–127, 141–145

Rén, 31, 128–130, 135, 162, 166, 176
Respect, 13, 14, 21, 52, 68, 69, 74, 81, 82, 84, 86, 92, 107, 108, 115, 117, 119, 127, 189, 190, 193
Rethink, 21, 26, 36, 49, 55, 56, 120, 135, 181, 184

S

Similarity, 14, 20, 64, 70, 77, 87–91, 103, 119, 123, 133, 135, 183–185, 191
Simplexity, 90, 172
Sky, 2, 68, 74, 84, 112, 120, 130, 189
Slander, 162, 163, 174, 195
Social justice, 4, 36, 50, 79, 104, 110
Soft power, 62, 63, 72, 189
Solidarity, 101, 103, 104, 118, 192
Starbucksification, 59
Stereotypes, 35, 42, 93, 144, 161, 162, 174, 175

T

Teaching, 49, 81, 91, 92, 117–119, 165, 191, 195

Togetherness, 20, 34, 62, 86, 101, 102, 108–123, 169
Tolerance, 4, 6, 21, 66, 77–79, 81, 96, 115, 119, 134, 136, 142, 190, 193
Translation, 17, 18, 29, 30, 43, 44, 49, 62, 84, 86, 89, 109, 110, 112, 117, 127, 128, 134, 138, 141, 163, 164, 166, 167, 175, 183, 187, 188, 190–192, 195, 196

U

Unity, 4, 15, 16n5, 81, 103–106, 109, 110, 115, 116, 118–120, 123, 192, 193
Universal love, 78, 83, 97, 190
Unthink, 21, 26, 49, 56, 120, 135, 181, 184
Untranslatability, 185

W

Western-centric, 5n2, 9, 180

Printed in the United States
by Baker & Taylor Publisher Services